THE COLLECTION OF TATYANA

THE COLLECTION OF TATYANA

THEPOETESS.

TATYANA ROSCOE

POETIC VISION.

" I want to be clear about this. If you wrote from experience, you'd get maybe one book, maybe three poems. Writers write from empathy."
- Nikki Giovanni.

"Less conversation, more demonstration." - Anonymous

T

The Collection Of Tatyana

Preface

The collection that took me twenty years to write. A journey that's filled with inspiration, motivation, love, fear, mistakes and God. I felt the need to be as authentic as possible. Which led me to My life's trials and tribulations. These moments created memories that shaped my mentality. These memories created the foundation for my current reality. This collection will go beyond judgement. This collection is a reflection for the unspoken. This collection is a breath of inspiration. I ask the reader to indulge these words patiently and creatively. I will continuously thank all readers for being open minded. Whether you know me, or was caught scrolling, I sincerely thank you for contributing.

My stories are real, they derive from a place of emotion and experience. Difficulty does emerge when an image does not appear with my words. I will admit that creativity tends to take a hold of me. If the image is not present, then writing becomes a feeling. I may write a poem with no meaning at all. When you read it back an image may not appear.

But, as I'm writing these pieces, continuously re-reading them. I begin to recite them obsessively, Falling in love with the syllables and pronunciations. Poetry is its own language. Rhythm and poetry, poetry has been passed down for generations. Poetry could be my first language. Please excuse me if I come off as repetitive.

I've grown extremely comfortable with how I choose to relay messages. Using the same words in different ways may be evident. The growth of my art continues as I grow as an individual. Even if my process changes one day, I feel the reader should understand that the purpose is to always evoke emotion. Creating a conversation about how the reader interprets the narrative, along with deciphering the writer's intentions.

I speak on this because I want my readers to know that I write from a personal place. Every word is my own, and the stories that may come from this collection are authentic. I hope that my readers are not left empty handed. Even though this journey is personal, I have high hopes that every reader will be able to connect.

One Last point, As I began arranging this collection, I truly became inspired. When I look at where I started, versus where I am now creatively, I realized I was the one holding myself back. When you come to terms with the fact that you're the reason why you're not chasing your dreams, it changes you. Do not allow insecurities to be the ruler of your kingdom. There's an abundance of light that always surrounds you. If you choose not to tap into your power, then you will not evolve. I encourage you to never allow another individual to block your shine because Faith is the only way to begin.

If I Be a Poet.

If I were a poet. I spit these rhymes every time, never stoic in my lines, sparking change with my mind. Blank canvases, I create on the dime. My passion is fine wine, my energy is inclined, positivity is the vibe. Never think twice, claim that title if you're nice.

Born in 94'

Caught in a drought but I stay reminiscing. I came to this world more different than they thought. Far from a loss, I'm calling it a blessing. I'm not supposed to be here, but my presence is evident. Never second guessing but my truth has been spoken. Actions and decisions have me standing where I'm supposed too.

Everything is written I'm not faking how I'm moving. Call it a mistake, but the proof is in the pudding. Speaking from experience, I'm connected, I really do this. Born in 94 as a girl who would question it? Checking out my stature, move back you can't handle it. All jokes aside I see you judging from afar.

Checking me out as I try to see who you are. I know it's surprising all this Power in my body. I know you like the fact that I came off so mesmerizing. I'm not trying to misstep; my life is the best. Getting Caught up in a jam does not defy who I am. Sitting back processing my essence and prowess. I am a big girl I can push through the crowd. The noise gets loud when doubt starts to creep around. Yes, I am proud. I'm speaking words from my own mouth.

Never embarrassed I stay strong through it all. Failing is not an option but a plan will break my fall. I'm Looking for a metaphor as I wait for my ride. A rocket just pulled up; I'll be landing on mars tonight. I'm moving on my own, looking out my Snow globe I want to be alone. Staying flexed up navigating how to be grown. Age is just a number, this is what they all tell you, certify yourself stay focused & keep it playa.

Prescriptions.

Questioning my quality of life, it's not right. Reaching for goals that I can attain if I try. Desperate for attraction, I'm sorry for even asking. I'm stuck with the mask Blending in with my sorrows. A witness to reflections, your girl is stating facts; I only recognize my half. Who am I exactly? My Reflections are cracking. Falling in line has my alignment losing traction. Falling in the gauntlet, guns aiming at me in this world I'm a target.

My spirit is earmarked for a reason I deserve it. Born to be unique, how I think is not a burden. Popping pills early in the morning to get me going. If I miss a day I will not live for much longer. This is how I was raised, taking steroids when I was younger. Complications as a baby, but I was much stronger. Naturally, Hormones and emotions came at me much harder.

Conquering myself and this world I've been different. I never ask for attention; I mind my own business. People cannot apprehend so they choose to stare instead. As I got older, I had to learn to be distant. Focus on myself and I'll handle any turbulence. Lessons as a kid taught me that nobody is perfect.

Breakfast at Night

I experienced the denial of a lifetime. Even as I speak now, I reminisce. Am I being dramatic? Was it that bad? I've grown tremendously from my past. Walking through fear no matter the result. Keeping my head high even if I'm last in line.

Learning not to attach myself to the outcome. The opinions of others do not matter to me. Embarrassment is not real if I don't care what other people think. The growth of Taty is the key. Understanding your own intentions in this universe is also key. Facing yourself before myself intervenes. What are my wants and needs versus my reality. I'm slowly shedding skin my past self is a casualty. My growth is riveting. Experience is teaching me; Epiphanies carry me out through the evenings.

Finally.

Good morning to you all, I hope you find peace. No matter your age I hope you're striving towards your dreams. No matter the day I hope your spreading good energy. Live with a Positive mindset and you'll achieve.

Compliment Me

If you feel the energy to say something, then please do. Your beautiful, intelligent, vibrant, heaven sent. I know these words may be foreign. You've never been lifted in such a way, I know it. Please do not hesitate, use your words if you're feeling confident.

My voice fills my ears, so a companion is welcomed. Even as a stranger, I never choose to judge them. I hope I do not come off as cocky that's not the logic. This world is too quiet. As I get older, I realize what I admire. Choosing to speak up even when it is not required.

In loving Memory

I found myself at the lake one day, looking in the water at my reflection saying hey. Fishing poles leaning towards the water steadily, ears and eyes watching and listening intently. Five in the morning bright and early catching something. I have to say that I've been dreaming about this day. I constantly reflect, these memories of my father are growing more intense. I know the message was heaven sent. Still till this day I try to decipher it, privately, he speaks to me. As an adult, the younger me is a travesty. This journey saved me, finding answers while I'm aging. The power is me, as I sculpt the details of my dream. My potential is supreme, the third eye is watching me as I Plant my seeds.

Loving myself because she's all that I need, the healing starts over when obsess obsessively. Hard to forget when you continue to reminisce. Losing someone in this world you can't imagine, but you'll get accustomed to the people that surround you. Losing someone is a pain not to be handled. I'm sure you get the picture, many years ago a young kid had it different. Pouring out her life in the abyss from a pitcher. There's nothing left, but a refill would reset. Present Opportunities to take new steps.

Visual Visions

As if I'm looking through the television, seeing colored images playing out in my mind. A world inside me that I do not understand. Silently conversing with myself under my breath. Their talking to me as if I understand oh god help. I'm stuck in a madness that I really cannot explain.

Seeing all these people holler out in so much pain. Words and voices spinning round' in my head. I'm filled up with guilt I can't tell you what I did. If They want me in a stray jacket they'll have to think again. I knew my father for eight years is he the one to blame? Four of those years I swear to God I can't attain.

My apologies for using god's name in vain. Say it isn't so, oh yes, she's so bold. As I get older, I feel the future is on hold. What I know now is that I do not have control. Still losing battles that I thought I would win. Quieting the chatter now I'm back on the go. I visualize my struggles and success in a bubble. Nightmares have clashed internally like no other. If I stay focused, I hope to see my purpose. Trying to help more than the hurt or the burden.

Freestyle.

Staying strong in defeat is something you can't teach. The decisions you make will shape your reality. Taking small steps, that's the motto, that's the process. Wondering what's next? Achieving goals without stopping. you created your own lens. Seeing dreams through your optics, optimism is the concept. Digesting artistry as I breath what it means. Living in this life it became an essential need.

Set You Free.
Your dilemmas are nothing compared to who you want to be, I admire your hustle, as you dip in and out of these streets. Taking care of your family while ignoring the misconceived. They're not understanding push them to the side, please. Distractions are building but you are looking straight ahead, whatever you're running towards man I hope you find it. A lot of people dream but misstep with the first step. Never had to act, so that reality is a missed trip. I must tip my hat because I see you're on a mission. Maybe I'll back up just in case I got you slipping. I promise it's never on purpose, baby I'm just living.

Enjoying conversations, enjoying your attention. Having you for moments I feel lucky let me mention. All I want to do is change your dimensions, why you may ask? Well, I'm the something that you're missing. I don't have the time to brag so allow me to finish. My reason may be a little deeper than intended. I yearn to explain but my actions will demonstrate it. Patience will lead to you being my lady.

T.R.A.N.S: The Real Affliction Now Soars.
In my heart, waking up, feeling like somebody else. I know it hurts, looking back I'm glad I made it through my past. Being Gay is ok. Always feeling judged? Well, hey, who are they? It doesn't matter anyway; I'm blessed to live in such a way. Bisexual, Trans or Straight, these words exist to help us communicate. Never let a definition define your ammunition. At the end of the day all you have is you. Looking in the mirror who's that looking back at you?

Random advice but you already know what to do. Scratch it from your mind the process you'll jump into. The reaction from your family, but this is the road to being happy. Always stay true and remember mistakes are few. The power of a choice will have you happy and rejoicing.

The road might be long, but you'll always learn from it. Life is a blessing living life is our purpose. Whether good or bad you'll proceed if you are hurting. Always love yourself and the blessings will show themselves.

A Toast to you...

I see how you've grown as I stand by your side. Watching you attain goals I'm Glad you can call me a friend; I just want to show support. Realistically this is your ideal world, I'd be lying if I said I'm not proud of you girl. Standing tall in your marriage, being proud of your heritage, walking in your shoes creating paths are you aware of that?

Giving birth to children on your own without complications. One boy and one girl there growing up in this world. I'm proud to say that I admire the way you demonstrate. I appreciate your struggles; Your presence is a rebuttal towards the pain from your past. How you made your way is what matters in the end. Moving forward is like the thoughts in your head. Nothing ever lasts and you've recognized the path.

Identifying with your higher self as you glow within your powers. Symbolizing strength, your roots are expanding like trees. Delicate and precious as I visualize a flower. My first impression was the silkiness of a rose petal. You're on a different level, I see the power that you'll breed. You're too exquisite, your existence is making time lapse I'm not kidding. I'm praising with intention, deserving of every mention. Countless lessons, you've received a message with these lessons for a lifetime.

You've always had this light, it never changed in your eyes. The motivation that it takes to make something of your life, you're doing things right. Even with one eye I could never be blind towards your accomplishments. Never complaining there's a method to the madness. All I'm trying to say is it feels good to be a witness. Doing the right things back then, now you're in position. A hustler at heart as you salute with intention. Minding your own business and making money missions. Focused on the family that's a rider's ambition.

Summer.

Needing validation is not a part of the game we are playing. Listening to you talk to me like a fool. I got caught Spilling my dreams to a small minded individual. Never will I forget the example you tried to pull. Snatching my dreams to benefit you in your world. Now I understand that there's only room for one. I don't care about the next girl trust me I'm one of one. Chasing my dreams has me taking strides towards the sun. My fingers are tingling, this feeling has me in awe. Hunting for a meal that could feed generations, my senses have been alerted since birth; I cannot waver. Following the foot trails and smells I'm in position. I'm ready to receive my gift like God intended.

Consistent Flow.

I still wonder what I do it for, rejected a few times but it's still not a blow. I know they could never understand the flow. Never giving up because it's all that I know. Eight years old discovering a new world. Creative in every way, even as a little girl. I've grown a love that raises me high above. Having good intentions while being genuine is white like a dove. Driving me crazy words haunt me on a daily. Artistic views, I pay attention to still amaze me. Different Outcomes of creations don't hold weight in the making. Going with the flow consistently is the haven. Having good intentions and loving what you're doing.

Mentally being in-tuned with every single moment. Letting your emotions touch base is so important. Like a memento you won't forget the tempo, laser beam focuses on direction and then go. Curated masterpieces like a proven thesis. Being great is not a challenge when it becomes your reason. Watching her as she moves, she is seasoned with the pen. Something so connected I could never pretend. Arrow to the chest Cupid shot me again. Running around never stressing about you. A conversation that will never be overdue. I'll be eighty years old still admiring how you move, Pursing forever with the creations between us two.

Divine Guidance.

Burning up my lungs, just another slow night. Made $100 but that's just something slight. Mapping out my plans and my goals moving forward. I'm done being optimistic I know what I'm here for. Never waste a gift, just commit to explore. You were born with it now craft it like a sword. Only certain soldiers understand the art of war. But everyone will not have the heart to endure.

No matter how high my inspiration got me flying. Learn how to stay true to the craft or You're lying. I walk in as myself, I'm not changing for nobody. Why would I bend my mind to follow your plans and not mine? Think about it, you'll commit suicide without trying. No matter the situation I'm picking up the pen. Communicating from within, I am writing out my sins. Writing out my love, emotions and dealings.

High off Life.

High off life opportunities got me feeling right. Take a stroll at night reminiscing about my past days. I was in a haze so foggy I could not gaze straight. Priorities on the waste side chasing the ultimate high. I had a girl call me out last night, that did not sit right.

It crossed my mind this afternoon while I was at the school. Graduation time, my niece made it through. Standing ovations as she walked that stage too. Distracted by my thoughts I made a move to the car. It's been a couple days, but I promised to change my ways. My emotions rushed in as if it was a wave.

Fearful of the situation, I see you've changed. I'm tired of playing games. I'm trying to save face. Run away with me somewhere far like the tropics. Trying to be healthy but this environment is toxic. Avocado toast, good sex, and the gym, now your regimen got you feeling good again. Being healthy is a trend but we all know your delusional. Sleeping with your best friend, you said on the low. His credit card is paying for that car note you owe.

Lost Generations

The same problems circle around with intention. Influencing the younger generation is a weapon. Knowledge is power and they use it for oppression. Now Different generations of races are being expressive. From police brutality, sexuality, and celebrities. Influence is everything even down to the financial things Look at how racism is so connected to our democracy.

Repeated bigotry is all connected to our history. Surviving while black in America is a reality. Looking at today these mentalities are superior. How can we reprogram these people to start hearing us? How can we derail a due process that was meant to put fear in us? Three fifths of a human was deemed legal in the U.S.

I'm always speaking facts as these white people lack in culture. They lie and scheme getting away with everything. Relating to the leaders with pale colors in their features. I hope y'all don't mind I added a side note during this time, I'm in my bedroom writing this line for line.

Black Hoodie

"Suspect walking down fifth and
Broadway wearing a black hoodie."
I know you're terrified and traumatized when you hear the news. Young Tyrone got two blasted in his dome. Whoever he was beefing with sent his ass home. Daily conversations of being protected in your home. Even when your child is walking late nights from school." Practice went over a few hours is that cool?"

"I don't have a ride, I spent gas money on food. I'm not tripping though the school is a couple blocks from you. I'll call you when I leave and text you when I'm halfway. Try not to worry mom I promise I'll be ok." Walking back home he stopped at the liquor store. I think we all know how this type of story goes. As soon as he walks in, he is being eyed head to toe. White man Billy Joe who buys those beers from the store. Always after four once he finished working next door. It's about six pm he is conversing with the clerk. Slowly Bringing his attention to Tyrone, "Sup Fella"?

Leaning on the counter with a cigarette hanging out. Tyrone's face is smug, being a jerk was the purpose. Bought an Arizona eyeing the blunts is it worth it? He shrugged it off walking to the door in a hurry. Left the change on the counter wasn't trying to count it. He had a bad feeling about this white man no doubt.

Cut a few corners so he could walk the back way. Crack heads and hustlers, prostitutes live in this alley. Walking with stride, head down, he has no time to waste. It's almost seven o'clock, the streetlights are turning on. His momma will trip if he's late coming home. Hollywood Jack the local hustler is on. Standing at the end of the alley looking strung.

"Young Tyrone my brother what's going on?"
"Do you need a couple dollars? Is your momma at home?
Question after question, Tyrone gave him a nod and kept it pushing. Neighborhood festivities, but the streets looked out for him. His daddy got life protecting the whole block for them. Head shot to a cop; he would patrol these young girls. Pulling over and picking them up as if they are cleaning house.

Young girls disappear while their parents are freaking out. Caught by a lookout in the alley, he pulled it out. The girl was so strung out all she did was lay there. He's grabbing on her head, forcefully pushing her towards the hood of his Benz. Pulling on her hair, it felt good in there. The lookout said "boss!" and the hood came marching. Slapped him across the head with a brick no joking. Long story short the whole platoon was bussing. Top stood right there waiting for his armored fate. Handcuffs on as they swayed his ass away. His father was a legend in these streets, people know the history.

Still Tyrone approached the end of the alley way and got shot down. The echoes had people scattering like roaches on the ground. The cops pulled up and not one witness was around. A dead body and a wallet were found on the ground. A few feet away they found his can of Arizona. Both officers acknowledge it would be a long night. Preparing the scene as they go address the family.

Broken Home.
Killing, robbing and selling drugs was not my lane. Grateful to this day because I never had to gang bang. No disrespect to those who do it to maintain. Blessings to those who grew up not knowing a thang. Just following the footsteps of generational pain.

Momma passed out from the pills & alcohol in her system. Daddy never home but you stopped missing him. The neighbor is the baby-sitter which doesn't make sense. Seventeen years old living life too fast, too grown for herself daddy got caught rubbing on her ass. When he does come home that's where his eyes attach.

She tucks us in every night and then goes for a ride. Either way it goes this is the life they live. Even when daddy is far away her brother is here. His mind is warped, fourteen years old exploring the back of her throat. Nothing makes sense anymore, I'm alone. A young girl living in a loveless home.

Burning Towers

I woke up one morning ready to be petty. Being nonchalant you pushed me towards nothing. Thinking to myself was there something being felt? Caught up in your act, looking for some help. Falling in a trap, I guess y'all call it love. Feeling all that bitterness building down all our trust. Maybe I'm just talking too much, but what's up?

Tell me what you feel and why you keep blaming us? A ballad continued I'm tired of my own poems. Lately I've been writing about you, I think I've had enough. Caught me in a corner by myself hugged up. Confused about what to do, I'm trying to improve.

I hate to point fingers, but you are breaking up the groove. You know I'm not a fool, the deck you are pulling from is empty too. Lately you've been blue like the sea no kidding. Causing waves of empathy, I feel what you are feeling.

Look me in the eyes, tell me what you see pretty? Just Grab my hand let me save you from distress. If only I could save you from yourself, you're a mess. I mean that with the best intentions, you still not getting it. I was placed in your life only for your reasons. Cashing you out wasn't that so why be demeaning? Even if that's not what you're seeing just be real. Why are you acting like your pinned to a wall. As if you're a calendar, changing seasons every month. Like a falling leaf changing colors through the fall. I hate to be rude but why did you even get involved? The sex is pretty bomb, but other things are going on. Your concentration is on track for your little girl.

Not a bad thing, I know she's your world. All I'm trying to say is that me and you are rocking back and forth. The boat is not steady, and I don't know where we're heading. It doesn't mean I'm regretting; I still wanted the wedding. Your decisions I still question even though you found blessings. I'm looking at you now, is this better than before? Just because you gained doesn't mean it equals more. I bet you didn't think this situation was in stores. I'm being blunt of course but I'm praying for you even more. I love you to death my heart goes out to you and yours. If only I could help but I guess you want to be alone.

How I grew to hate you.

Thank you for the painful memories, I hate you. Looking in your eyes as you lie to me. Memorized by the words slipping from your tongue. I slowly realized your faults, but I could not run. Desperation was the funk seeping through my soul. Self-awareness crept in like the morning fog. On and off for many years I bagged up my tears. I took accountability for the pain I created here. I apologize to myself for the pursuit of insanity. Nothing is everlasting, and that was not happiness.

How I grew to hate you was self-indulgence. Addicted to the possibilities, but you and I were not meant to be. Caught between Chasing fairytales and reality. I'll admit the front you put on had blinded me. You're not the only one to blame I played the game just the same. I held on for all those years just to say that I hate you. Nothing accomplished but I finally forgave you. Forgiveness was conquered but I still reminisce. Love was absent I still can't picture it.

My Path

Finding myself slowly started affecting my health. Reaching for my dreams might be books on the shelves. My internal is battling, the feeling is crazy. Knowing you're the best but your thoughts get you hazy.

Feeling so unsure so your actions haven't made it. Still a different breed there's no faking for the feed. Trying to find my way but I don't know what I'm doing. Leading my own path and I'm blind while I do it. Still, I am progressive, were in the revolution.

I am the revolution I'm creating my own movement. Creating inspiration, I'm just trying to be fluid. Watch me as I go, I was born to do this. Speaking confidence as I feel my spirit lift. Encouraging energies will switch a room quick. Being genuine is stepping with the right intent. Filled with temptation is also my imagination. Struggling with the outlook of what it means to make it.

Statements.

I could care less about your opinions. Last time I checked God told me that I am winning. The position of observer is so fitting for me. My goals and dreams will not involve your understanding. I laugh internally I cannot help but to be. Holding on to coattails is not my reality. Mental confusion about my future is the travesty. Talent is not everything, just the beginning of my dreams.

Creating something of my own is truly a given. Never apologize for the blessings that you're receiving. Even when the judgement is strong, I keep breathing. Ten toes down, kids are looking up to me now. Life has me high off bliss I see what's coming. Grateful for these lessons, my life has been different. Never count me out I was chosen for a reason.

The Light.

She walks around barefoot sometimes. She always got a cigarette but never a light. She lives in poor conditions, so a buzz satisfies. It's hard to justify when she wonders all the time. Looking at the floor in the alley next door. Struggles on her mind every day, every night. She wears Dirty clothes with dirty open hands, begging when she can.

Her teeth are so yellow they reflect like sand. Gritty and unusual smiling when she knows it hurts. Surviving on these cold nights, living in the city they do not care if you live or die. Suddenly optimism sets in her eyes. The sunrise is beginning to show face into daylight. People hit the streets, as she listens to the sounds from the shoes on the concrete.

Mesmerized by the crowds of people living in order. Distracted by the view, a young man offered her a few quarters. She smiled in surprise and politely asked for a light. He reached in his pockets and pulled out a box of matches. She grabbed it quickly as she moves with excitement.

Her hands are shaking as she drags the match on the inside of the packet. Warmth near her hands she reaches up towards her cigarette. Slow with the inhale as the gentleman waits patiently. He decided to let her keep the matches with a few dollars. Swift with his dismissal, he was gone with the wind. One cigarette ago she was on that nicotine high horse. Now she's back looking through the trash, talking to herself.

Fate.

I can't do what you do, Nigga I can't do it like you, Nigga I said I can't do it like you. A Nigga like me lost my ego humbly. Matter of fact I threw it out the window. As I stare at the birds gliding up above. A steady stream of creativity I'm in the middle of. Grateful for all situations, I'm grateful to the idea of another one hating.

A creative like me does not belong in that equation. I live my life day to day, consistently I pray. Planning out my own world domination one day. Eyes staring hard, shake them off me lord I'm different in all regards. The reputation of life is that it can be hard. I'm protected against these walls I'm armored up. Never seen a roadblock my journey is untouched. The story that is already written, I'm just living.

Fear is created when the unknown is invited. Looking at my perspective, I never said it was right. This life could be a lie, do not let fear control your mind or allow it to be your demise. Insecurities arise when you care about lies. Remember they are not you; They cannot do what you do. Your style is special, And Your blessings are forever.

Set The Scene

A place in my heart that is where we will start. Treat it like a mission on a journey we embarked. Hand in hand skipping like a fairytale prediction. On a red brick road this is Cupid's expedition. Words like commitment and forever, we will always be together. Trials and tribulations, arguing and manipulation.

Never knew if you could make it. Still yearning for your baby. Speak it into existence and maybe you'll be favored. Determination and persistence are the right behavior. And still, your steady missing. The connection had conviction, as a witness, the love still hovers at a distance. Sexually engaged, now your thoughts have changed. Reality stays the same & unconsciously you're not sane.

Looking for the change as disappointment shows its face. Looking for recovery I thought she was the one for me. Looking for my chin she knocked the ego and the pride again. Where do I begin, all these lessons showing sides again. Blessed for reflections the toxicity was magnified again. It might take a moment for you to be alright with this. Let it all go and continue your path. Take your L's and make sure to hold them close.

Be Gentle with me.

She said, "Be gentle with me please." Physically and mentally my history still gets to me. I made mistakes willingly; I like the feeling that it gave me. Never will I excuse the abuse I went through. As if I was his muse, a pawn that's been used. She was so confused, is this what love can do?

Talking about excuses that he continuously uses. Sitting on the stool with Tears in her eyes. "Why would my man choose to act a fool?" He wasn't even a cheater, just a beater with a coup, two-seater. He never did commitments we just had a situation. Of course, I tried to change him. Then That led to him physically putting his hands on me."

"Shacking up together but my name was on the lease. Running the streets until he found an opportunity. That man should write my eulogy acknowledging I upgraded his mentality. Charitable with my peace and essence I showed him everything. Now I'm venting to you as if I'm lonely and desperate. All I can feel is Pain flowing through my vessels, I hear my blood cells echo; I need help. I need a mask to mask this L that I took. I need a man to stretch my walls, what size do you wear? Like twelve inches on a foot, I need pressure down there. I like to stretch it out, my ass looks good in the air. Put your fingers in my mouth and pull on my hair if you dare.

Back shots from point blank will make me love it here.

Y.

You are running through my mind all the time. Complications are taking away from our shine. Steady arguing when the arguments lead to nothing. Head butting through our moment, this seems kind of funny. We tend to disagree because of our past it seems. I remember the first day you said that you wanted me. Going back and forth as we dig a bigger hole.

Egos are in the way as they tend to take hold. I don't know where to go if you leave my life forever. It's a lonely road when we lose out on each other. The companionship I once cherished went around like a Ferris wheel. You choose to believe that these feelings aren't real. What's the deal? You're acting as if we are in a movie reel. I know you need to heal; I know I need to chill.

Running behind you like a cat, independent in nature but still were attached. Looking for the alley-oop, you know I always catch that. Little metaphors to let you know where My heads at. Now I'm learning lessons, and you know you are the cause of that. Whatever happened in the past, you know I can't take back. Listening to your pain has me going half insane. I know that I've changed but perfection cannot be obtained. What's your reality? Let's take a ride so you can tell me. Don't do me like other people baby, will you help me?

Confetti.

False celebrations have ruined us. We sit at the mountain top as if we're untouchable Hand in hand, stare to stare. The secrets we hold lie within the glare. Too beautiful to approach so we exist beneath. The lust equals a rush that becomes our reality. Delusion begins to crowd our so-called boundaries. Still, I succumb to you between the sheets. Yelling & screaming, smiles are beaming, hearts are racing, heavy breathing, baby pleasing, Confetti falling from the ceiling.

Crumbling.

Falling apart, I truly didn't mean to push us this far. I'm going over my actions, it's tearing me apart. I don't know how this happened. Focused on the problem but where are the solutions. Looking for some answers on why I choose to do this. Acting like an ass, you really think I'm stupid. I made too many mistakes but the conversations fluid. We're going back and forth but the stress is getting to you. Pregnant as it is I really think we should cool it. Admitting to the fumble when I stumbled in front of you. Feeling like I'm trouble, the distance between us is needed to clear the rubble.

Never intentional, I wasn't trying to hurt you. Doesn't matter now, you're seeing the world through your view. Not even a dig I'll always keep it a hundred too. Maybe I should grieve, I can see that I'm losing you. My truth is on display, but I mean what I say. Never a debate I swear your words hold weight.

Crazy where we're at, moving to crestline but you're living in the past. I know this is my fault, I should have looked at you and passed. Instead, I showed you off back then like a hall pass. Never ending ideas of what could be our next play. Admitting to myself this could be our last day. How will I face the truth once our love fades away?

Minimal conversations about how stagnated we became. Gradually, your reactions towards me started to change. Losing value because I would never buy you a ring. Mentally all you see is material things. Five thousand dollars on your finger but the man is not enough. A marriage never occurred but he continues to pay it off.

Five years later and I still remember it all. He has no aspirations, but his children celebrate him. Struggling with your daughter by yourself on facetime with me. Expressing your resentment every time we speak. The life you chose wasn't satisfying your soul. Your children were the only reason you chose. Justin had the semen to help complete the mission. Reminiscing on bad decisions, the lies that you told him when I looked through your messages. Common sense, you were still fucking on women.

The penis was temporary, a tool that was needed. A breather is needed, killing sentences while the ink bleeds on the pages. Just remember I've been waiting but were not celebrating. Releasing all energies but honestly that was deep. The difficulty for me is accountability. Spilling my truth but its toxic inside too. The Oedipus complex was relevant in the time we spent. Let's take a moment to catch our breath, this next line may need some air. You were weak from the jump.

Passing out on the floor when my hands found your throat. Coming into my house breaking plates and throwing hands. I cheated on you so my wrongs I cannot amend. I will not pretend as if you will not read this. No matter your reaction I've always been prepared. Walking with my head high I can never be scared. Even your lies will be extorted in the end.

Sunflowers & Roses

I will present them to you this morning, The smile that will come across your face I can hardly wait. I look forward to this moment, I know we will enjoy it. sunflowers and roses, girl you deserve it, don't worry about the purchase it's the principle I'm proposing. It may not be the world but it's worth something. I can't explain the gesture, I hope it lights you up inside. The thought of an opportunity to show beauty through my eyes. Early mornings came in as I arrived to you laying. Your back was towards the door as you faced the windows, A dozen roses in hand as I tip toe in, planning for your reaction so you know its genuine. I laid them across the bed. Anxious for you to wake up so you can see them right there.

Sitting on the edge of the bed I hear voices in my head. Trailing off in thought as I think about us instead. A splash of color is what I feel when you are near. I wanted to show you physically what I mean. I brought this to fruition, so you know that it's real. Listen to my words, do not scoff at my intentions. Our principles should be the last to go missing. Still itching to be the best situation. I Cross my fingers and make promises I probably shouldn't. I want you by my side until I die, is that alright?

I want you on the same page as me in this life. Bringing it back, I'm tied down matter of fact. I love her to death; She completed my best self. Taking deep breaths and diving in you understand? A joyful interaction to accompany you as you are rising. Admire them with patience. When you turn around sunflowers will be awaiting.

Pose

Still images in this perfect Polaroid. She's too damn gorgeous to treat her body like a toy. Strictly business, the way she bent over more. From the side, "Flick", from the side, "Flick". I had to take a step back because she's voluptuous. Thick, for those who may be simple minded.

Staring most of the night I think I may have found it. A fountain of Chocolate, I am fond of this moment. Walking with purpose she put her hips in motion. Beautiful, please give her a promotion. We are toasting with the potion, now we're breaking by the ocean.

Standing by my side while her legs hold her high. She leaned against the car I could see the tattoo on her thigh. I pulled the camera out, the lens and her eyes connected with no smile. Snapping these pictures all I feel is electrified. Confidence all over her body every time. Thick nappy hair she's a goddess from the sky. She didn't say much but these words came right on time.

"Do you like the pose? If not, I can do more." Photoshoots in my parking lot started around four in the afternoon. "We've been lost the sunlight so we can move this to the room" Time to move locations I have a backdrop for you too." She happily agreed so now were on the move.

Hesitant to ask her if she wanted to take some shrooms. Walking up the stairs with my equipment in hand. I dropped my head down to see a crease in my vans. Her phone started to ring, she pressed ignore instead of answering. Mumbling under her breath as She sent a quick text.

She locked the phone and then switched it off to silent. After that distraction we approached my apartment. Key in hand, I asked her to unlock it. She turned the knob and walked in as we conversed about photography. Following her into my crib, I could not fathom. It took me a minute to realize what this is.

My reality. Blown away this cannot be happening. Walking her to the room, guess what happened next? Naw, I'll let you all assume. Maybe we'll resume and I can tell you how I do. She was so consumed, in tuned with the mood. Let me stop now before I get myself in trouble. Late night creatives decided to get comfortable.

Silhouette.

Slow moves, the way you're grinding on me I approve. Late night missions just for you. Sitting in the driver's seat waiting for you. Between arriving and anticipating your presence, my mind started treading the path of the imaginary. Standing there in an empty warehouse you're legendary. Lights all around the place are decked out.

Looking at you now your needs are met in that dress. Your assets are poking out I can attest that you're blessed. Excited for this lap dance in my head, let's begin. Before I could sit down, I heard your heels by the car. Opening my eyes as you swung open the door. Checking on your hair as your smiling ear to ear. Gracefully you slide in, foot on the gas we won't be seen until the morning.

Airbnb check in, we needed privacy. Arriving on the latter side, about an hour later I wanted to turn her insides. Apologies for the delay, I needed a smoke break. Plus, she needed a chance to check in with a friend. Relationship issues, anyway, let's begin. Press fast forward now she's on top of me. I can't even lie her body is mesmerizing. I would speak on her mind, but this is bad timing. This woman is Thicker than a Georgia peach and she's on top of me.

I promise to God me and her were not talking. I'm lost in the art of her backside arching. Do that damn dance show me what your momma taught you. I almost said thank you as my hands caress her thighs. It's dark enough in here so you can't see my eyes.

Sitting on my lap as you're kissing on my neck, you're on the right side, head leaning over as I follow your silhouette. Impatience sets in as I'm unclipping her bra set. Excitement in my chest, you're as sexy as it gets.

I couldn't even talk in this moment; I'm tripping over sentences. It's

Eazy, the way you get me. Hips calculating to an Eric Bellinger hit. It's only me and you and that's the consistent groove. Stuck in a moment I can't stop touching you, A body that's softer than cotton took me to the heavens.

Splashing Colors

Dancing together for as long as forever, sitting on the porch marinating in the weather. A field of storms but there's something to report. Soft rain droplets falling down in a pour. Soup and Hot chocolate and more are indoors. Looking at the scenery I'm enjoying my family.

Friends also gathered around the living room floor. Dominoes, twister, Uno, checkers and more. A family night out in the house let's explore. When we come together it's delicate like a feather. Appreciating the moments, it will always get better, holding on tight hoping it will last forever. Time capsules capture the stills from the camera.

A crowd of laughter you'll probably hear long after. Vibrant energies stemming from that cold beverage, were all adults here so alcohol may be present. The food is a blessing I swear it tastes like heaven. Home cooked meals, what do you think you know about it? Anybody in the kitchen for me just know I'm riding.

Wood stemmed candles burning in the background. Livid conversations starting to ignite now. Games are put away except for the one on the T.V, Lakers and Milwaukee. Different topics going on but we're all multitasking. Eyes going back and forth from the screen to the family. It's kind of funny, liquored up individuals started getting rowdy. Yelling at the T.V as if it's comprehending. Turning up the volume because they claim they can't hear it. Simplistic situations relating to your people. Reminders of beginnings before we entered this world spinning. Plans were executed before our being was manufactured. I see peaceful bliss; I'm always looking after this. Life gave me a chance to appreciate, do I deserve this? Either way we had to celebrate until the morning.

Moments with Kalahni.

A bundle of joy you are, your smile touched my heart. The effects of you have grown far. Your love marinates with the stars Unspoken affection; you gave us direction. Looking in your eyes I can understand the message. Mother Nature at her finest!

You were one hell of a blessing. I'm speaking as a witness, nine months with you and everything has been different. You've overcome so much, you've manifested possibility. Moments with you have shown a greater side of me. I love you always with your brother Zen Ray. I hope you both grow up together and make this world a better place. Teach each other lessons so both of you can become better.

Love one another and be kind, that's your purpose. You can't even imagine the possibilities we see. Your eyes give a shine, you're one of a kind kalahni. Remember that Nobody is better than one another. Work as a team, I hope you can stay out of trouble. You're adorable, I can't help but hold you close. You're 9 months old with a story of your own. Heaven's gates opened when you came out the womb. Now it's our job to make sure you fully bloom.

Messenger

You write this letter from afar, very detailed as you tell me who you are. I vividly remember how the eagerness came off. Straight to the point there were no breaks in your lines. I can tell you mean well, as you apologize. The bearer of bad news, yeah it gets you every time.

They say condolences as you burn from the inside. Trying to figure out how to hide what resides. Your tears run slow, and the numbness has arrived. The thought of a loved one not being by your side. Holding on to memories for the rest of your life. Looking at reality will become your insight.

While we're still here.

We act so fake when our people pass away. Showing love and showing up when it's too late. I understand life will find a way to intervene. Forget the excuses, pick up the phone and call me. Then we'll put our money together and order sushi. Struggling with chopsticks as were jumping through different topics. I heard you lost your car damn my nigga you, ok? Let's check i n on each other more. I'll Keep my ears close, so I know what you have in stores. Neither one of us is to blame, I don't participate in games. We'll converse one of these days to make sure we're on the same page. Remember to smile, regardless of what they say. Never forget, I'll be by your side always.

Grow some confidence and speak your mind through the bullshit. A closed mouth won't get fed; new ideas can't be spread. Don't be afraid to say how you feel. A part of growing up is knowing how to keep it real. Why be afraid when you make the decision to approach fear? Understand reality you can't even see it clearly. Fear is deeply rooted but the mind is not real. Hug him real tight while hugging her even tighter.

Love one another and smile through the trials. Believe in one another while looking out for each other. I love my brother, all my family, the first one being my mother. Nieces and Nephews, aunties even estranged cousins. Living in this life it goes quickly so be aware of it. Even when you slip, get up and learn your lesson. Appreciating your people through this journey is a major key. Believing in ourselves as we open our souls to humanity, loving one another is the main priority.

Wilted Peddles.

Dedicated to the ones who have come and gone. Inspiring us to live life all year long. Inspiring us to take chances even when were wrong. Never second guessing, thoughts will keep you stressed. Take some action and be receptive. Stay aware of the lessons as they disguise as blessings.

The same can go for second chances, nothing is for certain. Love everybody, especially the ones that are hurting. Shining through your personality, open the curtain. Be who you are open your wings and glide above. Let it be known that you are free to be who you want. When I pass on, I hope you remember me.

Pray For...

Fill in the blank this statement can be for anything, pray for the day, send messages to the universe. Pain crawling up your spine, to your mind, overtime. The weight of this world is slowly changing our insides. People having kids and breaking up in this pandemic.

People struggle by themselves and still can't get it. I'll pray for the nobodies hoping that gives you somebody. I know how it feels when you can't identify what's real. Praying for hope, the weight of this world is no joke. Thinking about the things that factor in, it overloads. Trying to carry more than you can, you'll implode. Impossible situations will have you running to the door.

Looped in these cycles, that's why we pray for. Mysterious diseases put the world on hold. Watch Them take their time to gain all control. Conspiracies unfold but this is just the world we know. This is how the story's told; The truth is not the end goal.

Manipulation for empty pockets they'll steal your soul. They'll work you hard, till your soles are black as tar. Empty hearts, seeing the truth is just as hard. How will it end? When all they create is despair. Their cutting off our air. Imbalances in our world and it's never been fair.

Dirty Sneaks

I Stumbled through the room with a Glass in my hand. An ice cube and Hennessy were about to be consumed. Smooth down my throat but my stomach had enough. I noticed the worlds spinning and I am standing still witnessing. I closed my eyes so I could start listening. I took off my jacket, I'm sweating hard on this balcony.

Black levies gripping my thighs is my style. Dirty sneaks on my feet beautiful and unique. Daydreaming fantasy as early morning peaks. Music in the background as the singer repeats. Drowning out the sound this liquor has me faded now. Before the hangover I enjoyed not being sober. The party was cool, alcohol was consumed. I took a deep breath, blooming towards success I feel blessed. Tonight was a mess, I stepped outside because the guests were simultaneously hurling out their stomachs. Dirty toilet seats will be the result of it. My apologies if that was too much information.

Fumbling through my pockets looking for a lighter. I saw a pack of matches in the kitchen an hour earlier. I should have grabbed them, a baddie walked past so I was distracted. A short attention span if only you can imagine. I have no choice now I must find a match. I've been here all day, I tried to spark a black but could not finish the play. I walked to the door and made my way towards the stairs, before I took a step, in walks that baddie once again to my left. Clutch in hand as she stares up ahead. Stuck in my stance I want to know her name. Hearts in my eyes I'm still standing here. She stops midway and turns halfway to a man.

He wrapped his arm around and grabbed her face to tongue her down. I should have known better. Allow me to get to stepping' before he notices my presence. Maybe he's a smoker, I want her to notice. Nah, let me stop, this party is over.

Duchess and White Owls.

Hard days I'm stressing, momma still protecting, I'm out here all alone going through chapters in my zone, mistakes holding me from my throne, reaching for the sky carry me home, last night alive, watch me make it right, marching to the beat, now I'm on my feet, even though I'm tired I still have strength in me.

I make it to the house and sit back on the couch. Pour the goodies out as I break down my last owl. Honey Dutchess has my spirit bouncing around. I light one up, Khalifa plays in the cut. Feet in the air shoutout to the recliner. Drifting with the high, do you think I'm high enough? Ash is building, I lean towards the tray on my right side, "Tap, tap like a cigarette. Leaning my head back after I took a whiff of that. Turning on my side inhaling every time. Safety precaution let me buckle in for this ride.

Girls and their friends.

Leaving class early so I can take a shot of henny. The homies at the house and that girl Cherilyn. I love Friday's as we approach the weekend. The plans are in motion as I hit on the potion. Stopping at the liquor store, too young to worry. Extracurriculars was the only priority. Jasmine the TA from third period met us in the parking lot. The rumor is she's messing with the homie and his dad. My boy Jordan, his dad is on the school board. Assistant principle, Mr Chef is how were supposed to address him. Anyways the liquor will be plentiful, Papers, blunts, backwoods and wraps, plus some snacks. Packs of gum and tic tac's, staying aware for when our breath starts barking back.

The females will be available, we have to stay fresh. Never get caught slacking, amen! God bless. Staying alert even when drugs are in our system. The party begins as soon as everyone arrives at the crib. Plenty of smiles and positive vibes, with no kids. The pool is in the back, so you know what this is. The first week of school starts back in August. The end of summer break is amongst us. Letting loose is all we intend to do.

Dank Exhale

I'm grown as hell now allow me to speak my mind. Going through these long days allows me to take my time. I need to vent it out, please allow me to get loud. Mentally or physically while I'm smoking or communicating. I prefer to roll a few but don't quote me though, I like to go overboard my mind is gone. No need to be alarmed, I've been a vet for so long. Roasting up my lungs there toastier than the sun. Just the taste alone is something so strong.

I like dedications so I had to give her one. Mary Jane, L's and reefer is how the slang goes. I promise I'm not a teacher, but the reefer got me teaching. Speaking in tongues, now im Ghandi for no reason. Colder than they know, under the influence or sober my words will freeze the world over. Imagine the reaction, that's not what their ready for. Accumulating, the growth now equals to a little sum. Honest expression, pay attention until you reach the credits. I was the next generation when the green had me caught. How can you ignore something that can't be taught? Mother nature's garden is so natural and flawless. Laying in the middle of my personal bud garden.

Smiling from ear to ear all up in my mind and, holding on to thoughts that get deeper in the process. Seeing life from different angles, blessings in your heart if only you can handle. Questioning what life is as I start to come down some. How can I regret the introduction on college grounds? I could go on, but I've been on this mound for a while. I'm enjoying an inhale, maybe me and you differ. Exhale while I'm talking on the phone to her sister. Toes on the rug while breaking down sticky green nugs. Dank aromas every time I light the blunt. Pen to pad during one of my own sessions. A mini vacation in my mind but I stay present. Eyes towards the sky, my destination has arrived.

Incense.

Sitting outside in my chair watching the garden. Music playing loudly, weed burning slowly. The sun is coming in over the fence as I welcome it. Faint smells of Sugandhalaya coming from the kitchen. The only thing on my mind while I sit back and unwind. Rewinding my day, I enjoy the peacefulness. Looking far ahead I always wonder what's next. Being very still I feel the thrill of my existence. These moments only last through the burn of the incense.

Hide me.

When you let yourself go that's your fault to you know. Who can you blame for the mistakes that you made? Is it a mistake? Or a lack of knowledge on our end, let's start a debate. Either way it goes you must live day by day. Find confidence and stand tall as you are. The realization sets in,

I know it can be hard. You're living in a temple, show some gratitude and learn to keep it simple. Take care of yourself so you can shine through your beauty. Appreciate the chance to say that you even knew me. That's the mentality so understand your unique. Embrace the mystic, as only you obtain this feat.

Professing & manifesting.

God is present as I count my blessings. I'm an entity I can't take that for Granted. One of these days I will be standing on a planet with my plants in hand, I 'm too Organic. To those who feel my presence, it's my purpose to address it. All odds against me but I'm floating to the heavens. Humbling beginnings that direction is destined. Everything I am I acknowledge it with no fear. Relearning is the path incoming messages are clear. The pain that I feel will redirect to the hills. Money isn't everything, but I know my time is here. Wasn't born on board but I swam and grew some gills. Adapting to the odds, this is who I am for real. Writing out my heart this testimony will go far. Reaching for the stars I'm literally writing to all y'all.

Take my hand.

I am a foreigner coming from the Netherlands. So far out you could not comprehend. Stumbling across different borders instills order. The idea of asylum has me on an island. No, I am not crazy, and I do not need help hiding. Yes, I am a foreigner to everything in front of me. I'm Locked in my imagination seeing possibilities. Tell me that I'm wrong for leaving the comfort of my home. The comfort of my shadow I've been hiding all along. Talking to myself as I say this with my chest. Tatyana, please go ahead and take my hand. Even this moment right here was always the plan. Trust your instincts and use your gift when it syncs. The revelation will free you instantly.

Twin

I see my days as they come their shining bright like the sun. One after another, looking forward to the pleasure of figuring out forever. These steps got me tethered. All my energy has come from getting myself together. This is my story line can you find me one better? I got it out the mud, detachment from my mental. I'm still the same me, my focus was perceived. Now I'm looking through seeing A twin that is me. I am aligned and in sync.

Traveler.

She navigated articulation for me, telling me things I need to hear while I breathe. Dreaming of a world that's an attainable reach. I had to take a seat. Losing touch with reality I plan to always eat; My stomach looks like dialysis; My spirit is on fleek. While I Actively flip this green, I'm working hard to be free.

Inherit

I inherited a village of opportunity. My people before me sacrificing all in unity. Pushing boundaries with hope to change our future. Now I face the world as I battle even further. Our actions are always worthy in the eyes of the beholder. All these white faces judging me that shit is over. All these revolutions, how many more do we need?

Asking for permission when this is our legacy. We were the first seeds to sprout into amazing things. Living as a minority I have every right to be. Unique within my character living righteously. The mindset of white people is twisted beyond belief.

But morally I'm sound and I could never make peace. We inherit this strength from our ancestors with ease, I could never find myself on my knees begging please. Looking in the eyes of these monsters before me. Knowing they aiming to kill us with just one squeeze.

Black Haikus.

Our first birth pushed our backs against the wall. Still sunny days with clouds forming a storm. Smile all the time with a high sense of pride. Political correctness slides down our backside.

Black Haikus.

We identify the pain, a community hurting again. Cut from the same cloth I guess I'll approach you like this. White supremacy, they will do what they wish. Living in this tribe, society has been the same ever since.

Black Haikus.

Twenty-Five to life he gave up all he had.
Guilty or innocent, the judge wasn't feeling it.
Life without parole, he's afraid of what he'll endure.
Walking down the line, grown Men looking in his eyes.

Third Leaf

The foundation is clear, I'm growing strong and direct. Enhancing chemistry's As I grow close to myself. Fine tuning my lane I'm in tune with the plan. Intuition is advanced I'm not too far out of bounds. I'm steadily making my rounds, but this circle is profound.

Repeating many lessons but there is a turn around. Accepting all these blessings but I wasn't changing routes. Looking at my present I can't punish myself now. Looking at the present as enlightenment shows its presence. Understanding patience, my third leaf has been waiting. My third leaf is elated it was raised with foundation. Deeply rooted, that's why you see the elevation. The work is on the soil so please have some patience. When I emerge, it will be with no hesitation.

Soaking up the sun and the water that God gave me. Nothing is ever perfect this is a cycle that we're claiming. Even when I'm wilted, I bounce back the next day. Too much of anything will have you despised either way. Life is full of decisions or choices you must make.

Once you find that balance then maybe you will be sane. Who's to say you're wrong when it's a feeling you can't shake? Who's to say their right when you fail in different ways? Never validate the opinions that they create. Stay with your third leaf, Foundation is the key, consistency repeats. The work is in the soul and that's who you want to be.

My Brother's Keeper.

I can admit that you tried to bring me in with your friends. The memories I have seem endless but then again, that was your world, I struggled to comprehend. Never been a player even though you threw the alley-oop. I caught it very well she was in the jacuzzi too. She dropped me off at home, ready to bone, but my attention span was gone. In love with a girl, I lied to her from the jump. My high school girlfriend was not bad enough. She wasn't gay either that realization was kind of tough. Tragically romanticizing what was not for me. I know you wanted to help me, but that girl was my habit.

I should have kept it locked, too young to be locked down. I should have had options, hanging out with k's younger brother I played both his hands. Girls at the school questioned me about what he was doing. These are the memories that come to mind when I think of you. Envious of the bond that you have with your father too. I thought that me and you would be closer, we both lost a parent. Close in age I thought you could understand who I am. Pushing off from rage that never solves anything. I wrote this collection to express all my pain. Nothing is personal, this is the art that I bring. Pulling out the roots that intertwine with my being. Part two can be seen, please continue reading.

My Brother's Keeper. PT2

I love your essence M.R D.R.N. My kin, my friend, you were too young to be seen as a father figure back then. The holes in my memory weaken me. Struggling to understand the meaning of our history. The meaning of our family tree, broken in so many ways we struggle internally. Still till this day fake smiles cross our face. Our people call it life but it's unfair in many ways. Grateful to your wife for the sacrifice she made.

I am writing this to you now because I know you understand. Continue to Live your life and fight for a chance. Do not give in to the sins between your ears. Feeling those withdrawals, but it's all between the ears. Ninety days from now it could be in your rear. Speaking from the heart I know I've tried throughout the years. Recently I've realized that I'm on a different tier. Seeing through my fears, I can see I'm out of here. Comparing situations is not the answer for you either. Call me a hypocrite, I know my journey is slightly privileged. Either way we know the language of addiction.

White In the Water.

Financial disadvantages will kill you if their able. The freedom in this country has a bullseye on our backs. Even after the dress shoes stepped on my ancestors like step stools. Reaching for wealth in a system that looked at us like tools. The wealth that was created from generations of old white fools. Families that were cracking the whip on our great, great, great. These people celebrated slavery and being the superior race.

White in the water somethings out of place.

Even through it all look how far we have come. Congratulations judge Ketanji Brown Jackson. You won the voting for Supreme Court Justice in historic fashion. No matter the timespan we celebrate our people. God Bless America the distractions were so evil. Did you watch the video? Did you hear the words that were said about the most qualified individual? Black as she can be, and her melanin took the heat. Tears stream down as she plays in the devil's playground. Old white men with blood rushing to their faces. Her mind is gold they could never take that away.

White in the water, the plan was already in place.

Bulldog.

Walking through the door as you roar at my mother. When I was I younger You two would argue with each other. This is nothing new, but this time you used abuse. I ran up to you with two fists but that was it. A few hits to the back and you pushed me down. Hunched over as you put your hands on my mother. Her face was soaked with tears of remorse.

Her back was against the wall as she sat on the ground. His voice echoed the hall as the night led into the morning. My mother begged me to stop fighting for her. I can hear her screams now as hands were put on her child. The disbelief in her eyes as the guilt started to rise. The relief came in time because he realized he crossed the line.

Modus Operandi.

Changed behavior is a constant navigator. People don't understand that their environment has raised them. Never can you hide because your past will show its side. Your method of operation shows a difference in your mind. Even if you're doing right. People tend to blind your sight.

They'll tell you how to live your life. Help you when your monies right. Their thoughts are in the clouds with material things. If you don't have it, then opinions start to spring. Living in California minimum wage is a thing. Paying you bi-weekly & slaving you cheaply.

Then there's education. How their validating debt is truly crazy, but amazing. One vote from the board and I bet the schools would change the rules to admission. People need to start having these conversations. She received her master's degree, and now she is writing her dissertation. Man, that's amazing! Personally, I could take some more classes. Connect at the center where students follow their passions. Creative thinking, when something pulls you in so deeply.

Higher learning is information that I am knowing. Thinking realistically who can survive on six-hundred dollars? Talk about saving but necessities always weigh in. Talk about a strategy, let's create our blueprint fam. I understand plans fall apart when responsibilities are to the brim. Stay in this moment and always tread ahead. Ignore all the doubters your talent has been bred. You'll never be perfect some things will never make sense. You'll always be worth it. Put effort into your purpose, this will get you further. One step at a time, one step at a time, it's working.

T.

Working a nine to five just trying to make it right. School loans and bills up my ass real tight. Cutting corners just to make my dividends right. Helping my sister to raise three kids they got needs. Making decisions and delegating I'm still learning. Putting my best effort forward has been the reward. Still hoping for the best as I shuffle through my stress. Hands to my chest as I lay and rest, praying to the highest. Wasted so much time being defiant I was trying. Looking for the logic in my actions as an adolescent.

Ducking and dodging the consequences now I'm present. Blessings coming directly to me straight form the heavens. Watching as my third eye awakens it sends a message. Supposedly I'm still headed in the right direction. Knowing what will happen before it lands will curse you. Walking this earth being unfaithful is a burden. Who I am today stemmed from a dark place. Seeing tomorrow is not promised, I advise you to stay in the present day. Only give thanks when you can see yesterday. Mentally living in the future is not a healthy state. Technically it's really all made up in your brain. Nothing is real except the present moment.

Divinity.
The whisper within the whisper. Catch it quickly before it withers away like the sand in Nuweiba. Internal conversations are becoming clearer and clearer. A bible thumping lesbian is not the idea. Praising the divine is the reason I am here. I cannot find the glory in pages written by man. I tend to lift my head and look towards the sky instead. I close my eyes and dream freely in bed. I step outside and breathe in the fresh air. I teeter on the edge of living right or left. Steadily Thinking I'm destined to be different. I've said it with my chest, but fear has been my witness. Walking with faith is something I never envisioned. I had to grow up to understand how this was written. Following your heart is the place of divinity.

Infinite thought.

Never ending,
Blissful understandings,
Standing as one,
Centers don't run,
Nature has begun,
We elevate towards the sun,
Harmony will be,
Uniting equally,
Can we be free?
Questions of infinity,
Silent thrills,
Are we even here?
Thoughts become ill,
Views from a hill,
Views from a cell,
Views in this hell,
Views in racism,
Whiteness I'll tell you.

America how dare y'all? Politics I'm unaware of, speak your truth, don't be scared! Don't you run! Please be aware, Feel the stillness in the air. See the change every year. Once again, I am here. An existence that's unfulfilled. Existing in infinite energy Searching for endless thrills.

Me VS You

I love you. I understand why the support is minimal. Pushing your objectives on me is criminal. Open your eyes please, I am a different animal. Throw me behind bars and I'll come out a scavenger. Throw me in a child's dream, I'll be mike from monsters inc. All I'm trying to say is that I can turn into anything. I would not doubt me I will be winning like Winnie. Watch me build a brand with a symbol like Nike. If only you knew me, you would have known that this was coming. I talked about phlebotomy but that was about money. Now I'm chasing dreams, but you worry I won't succeed. Part two is coming soon allow me to let this breath.

Honesty.

Sitting in my Chevy smoking within the tint. God respects the ones who work for it. Never question blessings, I promise you deserve it. Never question lows, keep your head up the days will continue to flow. Keep your head up, I promise the sky is reachable. Doubting your abilities will have you not reaching your goals. Trust me I should know, but That's in the past though. I'm running at full speed, rattled by hunger I've mastered my agility. Reaching over peaks and valleys consistently. Staying true to the craft I've gained some flexibility. People strut their stuff begging for a release. Knowing in their hearts they're not who they pretend to be.

Track & basketball

On the court playing defense you did not want to see me. I'm doing Track & Field landing in the pit you feel me. High school days it was crazy back then. I just wanted to ball with a stand of cheering fans. The idea of the sport meant everything to them. Even if it was only our parents' clapping hands. As a young teen it didn't really matter who was there. If you had a poster with school colors, you're a fan. This was the motivation that had me balling out of the gym. I was only 5'3 but standing tall like 6'6. No, you could not guard me ducking charges with assists. The refs hated me because your girl never missed. Watching intently making calls all night long. A young phenomenon with a focus that was flawed. Always been athletic playing sports was genetic. Won a few awards but my head was not in it. How can I forget the opportunity presented. Don't think I regret how I finished when school ended. Life comes with reasons and I'm happy just to be here. Cherishing all those moments that happened in past years.

The Poetic Story

"Just walk with me to the top of the hill." You know I have work today. Either way my boss is going to kill me. I just need a quiet moment with you Mya, do you feel me?"

Mya replies, "yes Elijah, I feel you.
Once we get to the top, we'll have a clear view.
It will feel as if we're on our own little pedestal.
Prestigious statues looking down on the valley."

"Oh my god Mya you're killing me with these scenarios. I will admit you can be very poetic though." Elijah and Mya started to exit the vehicle. Parked on the curb in a residential neighborhood. The hill supposedly has the best views in town.

Elijah never wanted to visit until now. They preceded in a consistent stride. The silence between the two is a commonality. Their comfortable & compatible. Nothing else seems to matter in this moment. Intertwined fingers as they walk in the morning. The silence still lingers even as they find enjoyment.

Jumping over the Horizon

I'm chasing my gift consistently. I'm in the process of creating my own history. A master at heart, I was born a work of art. Trust me if you can, I'm always working hard. Leveling up my skill while educating myself, and having knowledge is a thrill. Gearing up so I can climb every hill.

I see myself at the mountaintop sitting still. Experience will boost me in ways I used to fear.

I know a day is coming I will boast in their ears. Finding new meanings on what it means to live. Standing on the edge of the cliff, I'm taking risks. I'm Jumping over the horizon, into pure bliss. Never mind the people that made me feel diminished. Switching into multiple gears just watch me finish.

Blowing out brain pieces.

Let's rewind one time as I tell you about the sunshine. Early mornings on Saturday, playing ball at the park, "we got next! Check ball." Niggas running all day long. This is where I want to be. Living as a black man observe my history. Jamal is the name and I have a perspective. The devil was looking in my eyes Last Night. The feeling was so vile. Running my mind wild. I pulled out the pistol to his temple, it was nimble. Walking back alleys with my Patna' smoking reefer. Found out he was fake; So, I had to get him. Flashbacks controlling my mind as I unwind.

Stepped in the shower as I Steam with the water. Relief hit me deep as I focused on my daughter. No, were not blood, but I took care of her father. Low life piece of shit killing baby mothers. If Only I could see the sunshine, I still love her. Balling on Saturdays was taken like the holidays. Now visitation is where my daughter plays. Broken brown eyes when I went away. The consequences arrived after sunset. My very first night I heard the sky wept. I woke up in the morning next to a diamond. My room was lit up from the sun shining in. I knew she would appear; My sunshine is here.

Young Generations.
Give me substance. I want goosebumps on my skin. I need to feel the heat on me like a rug burn. Turning you over under the covers, now it's my turn. If you leave me for another that'll give me heart burn. Searching for sensations so I can make the world turn. I put my hands together as I pray to stop these senseless crimes. Brothers dropping dimes while having the nerve to be insensitive to their own kind dying.

Flexing these weapons, cars, women and money. Mentalities are empty tell me what you learned from stunting? Don't let those people catch you outside while you're fronting. They'll catch you in your town, clown on the gram when they get your ass down. I wish I could make this up. They'll plaster your video on YouTube now acting tough. Bullets to the face as they celebrate. Podcasts sharing stats like broadcasters too. If only it made sense, but this is the new genre of news What to do? A new world is on the loose.

Vaginal Gifts.

Your body is changing but still you look amazing. Born to create your process is respected. Lifting you up as a Queen knowing you deserve it. Looking at your scars and your tears, I can see your hurting. A delicate situation, connecting with other mothers over time fed your patience. Learning that your journey may take longer than the others. Noticing your struggles which will lead you to discover. Be gentle with yourself because this world can be clever. Designed to break the weakest people turning like a blender. Self-realization is life turning its own mirrors.

I know it can be hard wishing you could start from zero. Living as a mother you will always be the hero. Designed to be a vessel sacrificing something special. Battle scars present don't let it define your mental. Chosen for a reason your legacy is forever. Envy is the season all women cannot bear children. Saluting your commitment, your qualities make you perfect.

Chosen for a purpose just zoom in on your focus. I know struggle exists, but you have to keep going. Stillborn and miscarriages will never be ignored. A situation that will truly dissipate your soul. Causing more pain and confusion in your core. You could never imagine being involved with one of your own. Understand your loved ones the journey has been formed. Exchanging energies so a footprint can be born. Patiently waiting for the person that's to come. Approaching new beginnings is like a new horizon. Speaking from the heart, you also play a part; You are the lifeline. Guiding the younger generation into their own life. I can't define you; You have a right to live your life. Embracing motherhood and its struggles is only right.

Flow With Me.

I put these words on a page like a diary. I'm on this platform so you know it's meant to be. Food for thought, let me think, let me see. I'm talking to my people, so this message is melanin deep. Mixed with creativity just listen to my message please. Our people are dying in these cold streets. As you all know, our history with the police. As you might expect, I couldn't speak without divulging. The elephant in the room that refers to the times were in.

I recognize the movement so let me speak while I have the chance. Shining light on this situation, how will it change the land? I cannot say for sure, but I'm hoping for the best. Prayers fly high for all the sacrifices. I can't even lie; Our people are in a crisis. The revolution will be televised, giving praise to Gil-Scott but do you recognize? Boom, boom, boom, boom, boom, boom, boom seven times. 'Prayers up for Jacob Blake unfortunately we saw it live. This energy will stay alive! Were aware of our rights, but still their aiming for our life. Who's the representation? where is the explanation? Killers of the flower moon, their goal is to extinguish. I know this is not right, look around the next time you find yourself outside. The pain in their eyes, I hear the fear in their cries.

Middle fingers up to the pigs coated in filth, Even as I speak my mind it is what it is. I salute the officers who do it right regardless. Skin color should not matter, what happened to that badge of honor? Serve and protect but my people are being slaughtered.

Posting
What are you looking for? Who are you looking for? Half-dressed snapping pics, topless, showing D**k. So explicitly, I need to take a breath and think about this. Reading timelines our generation is in a crisis, a lot going on and the attention is strong, new communication, still in the making, man it is crazy, what you been doing lately?

Online dating? Instagram playing, tweeting every day and, I can't even say it, who are we impressing? Show a little discretion, that facade you are showing isn't really that important. Stop spilling your emotions, these people barely know you, and even if they do, your business is not to be pursued. I know I sound rude but my observations I conclude.

R&R

Skipping rocks at the lake at a park in December. I should of went fishing but I left my pole at home. Standing on the edge as I breath in this cold air. Clearing my head as I feel the breeze on my skin. Inhaling oxygen in a natural environment. Grateful for these days I get to live in such a way. Rich at heart but money is not everything.

Raising kids now but they don't belong to me. I'm Loving me in such a way, I think it's destiny. What did I do to deserve this opportunity? Praying to God with honest intentions, just you and me. Always mentioning that, I'm grateful for the light you bring. Growing in different ways I can see I'm manifesting. Taking the time to reflect on this life is not an accident.

Leading Through the Storm

I push farther into my life's stride, always keeping my head high. Going through these cycles I couldn't even tell you why. I know I stay strong even when I start to cry. Tell me what you think is going on in this place of faith. Mentalities can't even move with grace through their darkest days. No matter the struggle it's always powerful to live your way. I know a lot of things can disrupt our emotional state. Understand that life is an ongoing wave, we're slapped against the rocks then we begin to find our strength. As I fight my own battles, I am familiar with that pain. Never derail, the storm will calm once again. Umbrella in hand, I cannot get caught in the rain.

Aware

Life in general gives me a scare. I'm done with the bare minimum I'm aware. Waiting for my blessings but they've always been here. Opportunities are present and i'm starting to take advantage. The silence from her lips speaks, trying to decipher why she wants me. All alone in these streets wishing for a little care. Who would even care, this is all my own doing. Growing up unaware in the public school system. Diseases in my system, addicted with depressed days, anxious for a new way. Thanking God as I pray, I'm always hopeful in his grace. I had to lay it straight, being honest is ok. Searching for better days as I vent my pain away.

Adapted.
Looking in my mirror as I try to understand, I stumble all the time, but I always seem to land. Adapting to the struggle has been my only command. Never falling off I see that as an accomplishment. Growing a few inches will be my past tense. Living in the present, I don't think I'm there yet.

Never afraid to fail because God taught me well. Time traveler, I remember all of those years. No matter how long it takes, I'm still standing here. Flexing up I'm processed, never going back in steps, keeping my head up and staying focused on what's next. I've adapted to harsh realities. Living as a kid I was already conditioned.

Now, I'm in a place where I can learn and take it in. A twenty-twenty twin nigga, you know that type of grin. I flow through life being aware of situations. I flow through life, always grateful for my placement. Appreciating humanity at its essence. Understanding, none of us were born with directions. Working at being the best me while I'm living. Doing what I love because that's the only feeling. Recognizing emotions when the feelings begin to rise. I Grab it by the core and deal with it on the side. Don't be afraid to give yourself some time. If you're not mentally stable, it will kill you eventually. I promise that's coming from a real-life experience.

I promise this is me. Writing versus that will one day reach New Guinea. I promise to God, I will always continue teaching. Giving information, y'all know I'm never playing. Get on board and engulf yourself, let's explore. Adapt to this world and find the tools to make your own. Self-discipline is something we should all know.

Nepotism.

There's a conversation brewing among my people and our children. Gentrification and buying black are connected in many ways. In twenty-twenty four I think it will become a movement. Nepotism, just let your people buy exclusive. Never leave your neighborhood without buying influence. Fifty-five years later and our people own less property. The end of segregation brought an end to our communities. All-inclusive black businesses in major cities. Money was even taken from the negro leagues.

All I'm trying to say is these facts hit me deep. Our people rather sell to the rich white man. They did not take the time to talk it over with the family. Now we look around still fighting for the crown. Looked down upon like insects on the ground. Social media helped our words get back around. Now the rich and famous are educating new players. Supporting and motivating by spending their own money. What about the NFL and the Super Bowl controversy. Hashtag #buyingblack, yeah were on that.

Supporting small businesses, black owned we are witnessing. Nepotism should never be up for debate. How could it be bad for our people to share things. We need to keep it like the year nineteen sixty. Now we're starting to build back our communities. Segregation was supposed to be our birth of nations. Unity brings a presence that's filled with this essence, to always stay together. Our percentages are low so please don't forget the message. This present day in age our people slightly lost their way. Nepotism is present so we'll continue our generations.

PTSS
(Post Traumatic Slave Syndrome.)

Something that's in black people. Suffering together because they know we're not equal. Past generations know the d'evils in white people. Current Millennials selling souls to get even. It's all about the paper, so you're choosing to leave your people. It becomes much harder to be better, when the cheddar has you feigning.

You're starting to feel all the Percocet's and pills, Codeines a thrill. Thinking that you're cool but your people suffer still. Slave mentality blatant disgust in our society. Post Traumatic Slave Syndrome is in mindsets. I know it's a mouth full, but I am trying to be direct. White people set this world up so they can win.

Now they are using young black kids for destruction. Creatively Hip Hop is everything to me. Driving down the street seeing a white kid bumping meek. Who the hell is he? How can his lyrics connect him to anything. This is what I'm seeing, I want us to stand for more. P.T.S.S. is in the middle of our core. This slave mentality is being used more and more. Open your eyes, the race card is still alive. This life is a game of chess and unfortunately, we're still the pawns.

PSA: Blacker.

I ate some fried chicken last night. I couldn't tell you why, but I was playing curren$y and

Jay Z in my ride. I have dreams of marrying a black woman with pride. So much pride you'll always see my wife with an Afro at all times. You'll hear the speeches about our people being murdered. Police brutality and how the world is filled with negativity. Especially against people with darker skin tones. This world is cursed with a sickening, but still, you see me. Someone may say I hate my country. Maybe for reasons different from what you were thinking.

The principle continues to sit within. It's not the actuality you can't just make amends. When I create these collections, I have a message. Never can I forget how black I am. Never will I ignore how black I can get. Trust me, in the end it all makes sense.

We're not from this world and I've been convinced. So much hatred for what? It will never make sense. Even when I read our history the white man is just sick! Judging our culture and world off imagination. It's demeaning how they turned to domination. Then again this was just a message.

Holding a Black fist in the air, forever.

By Design.
My father, my Granny and my uncle died. These tax brackets got our money kind of tight. The state getting paid from incarceration. These places still allow modern day slavery. Inmates get paid less than ten cents a day. Families on Section eight receive incentives for the father to stay away. Living on these grounds, the blood of a slave helped the trees start to sprout.

China Loaning money to Africa is a trap. Buying up their land in government acquisitions. The rich are getting richer, the poor are getting poorer. As the years go on, I can see their true colors by Design like no other. Self-educated I discovered a plethora. Trying to spread the message to my brothers and sisters.

Even if you refuse to listen, I will still be here. One day my words will be speakers to your ears. You will not be able to refuse what you hear. I'm steering right now but soon I plan to switch gears. Slightly off track let me switch back.

I horde ideas that's a real fact. These Generations saw the horror in their order. Racist Caucasians manipulating through the seasons. They just arrived here; I think they date back about six thousand years. Was it by design that God had us mistreated? In the next life we'll be living like we're equals. Never question fate, these obstacles give us strength. Living in an unfair world, why would we break?

Even when were at the center of attention as a race. Clearing my mind as I write to you today. I wanted to check in, now let's focus on the next line. Everything is designed our spirit cannot be inclined.

Keep moving forward, always looking for the light. Catch your blessings because they're coming all the time. Understand the lesson, self-manifestation is something that is a given. Thanking the one above for these words that I've written.

Emmet Till

Back in the fifties racism was the politics. A superior race dictated every argument. No matter the place or the evidence pending against your case. Violence was safe, as they cheer early morning thrills. Walking outside just to see our body hanging from that tree. It's a disease how they can treat somebody differently. We're one in the same, poisonous thoughts Implanted in our brains.

A white woman is too good for a black man. A black man will just infect her with that color shit, other shit, willing to kill to make a point of it. Do you think we're not eager to kill because you raped our women? Illegitimate children are being denied because of color. Disgusting white women lying on our black brothers.

They never saw age, nor did they have any compassion. They were filled with hate which evolved into rage. Doing what they wanted which was murder until this day. Nothing is justified, the things they do are not right. Examples still occur look at the Central Park five. Injustice in America, watching us closely they will continue to stare at us.

Many discussions have been had, but they're still scared of us. They'll set us up real quick while using nigga in a sentence. Officers fearing for their lives while writing tickets. Driving while black, be careful they might get you. Living while black is another issue we still have. Until the day we die we'll be Dressed in camouflage, ready to combat. Think about the bodies in the ditch piling up outside. Set aside your pride to load up that four-five. Swallowing my pain for the rest of our lives.

New whippings.

Let me let y'all in a bit. We stay in politics bringing up new topics. We'll sway from the government, focused on other things. Starting to dwindle in, gone from my mind all this work that I'm putting in. Receiving these checks, but my dividends do not advance. Save a couple bucks but there in my pockets man. How can I exceed a thousand dollars in two weeks?

Get another job working hard on my feet. America is pimping every part of my body.

Taxes are getting deep; How are they taking all this money away from me.

Never will I complain I have visions past the planes. My pockets will keep growing this work does not hesitate. Focused up ahead, my thoughts just let them rest. Put those words to bed this life is bigger than a test. Acknowledging new whippings corporate companies create the system. Government officials pass bills that are legal. Watching people work for years to get even All this corruption that is public leaves me speechless. Anything worth going for comes with consequences.

Money.

"More assets, less objects." Shout out to the "Earn your Leisure" podcast for expanding mindsets. Watch me push the growth of this process. I'm trying to teach my people the importance of wealth in knowledge. Deep diving by myself while I sit with a pen and pad. Writing down a list of goals for the years that's ahead. My family has been the foundation, the motivation for the change in faces. So, where are y'all at? Building your own empires but together we're unmatched. It has been set in stone; How can we build brands on our own? Financial literacy should not be foreign in our homes.

Desensitized

The United States of anxiety, it might sound corny but it's true in America. People get extorted everyday like their playing chess. Kids smoking cigarettes and also having too much sex. Babies popping out to the right and the left.

Girls continue to shake their ass for the gram. We had a president that was a racist. He was living in the white house, and this is what I'm saying. He Said things that should never had caught this much attention. Reading through the paper there's always a headline. Political conversations are far from where my head lies. Desensitized to America in general. Think about the actions that have been done to other people. I stay in this world racism is pure evil. Black men, women and children are getting shot down it's a sequel. Racist white cops shedding bullets in my people. My people still killing each other to get even.

Compassion doesn't come from the shooter but from the victim. In recent memory I can pull from TMZ. They took advantage of Nipsey dying in those streets. Videos plastered everywhere like it's for marketing. The world was desensitized to that man losing his life. All I'm trying to say is sensitivity is slight.

The world knew about it in less than 24 hours. The World Trade Center blew up on channel four. A six-year-old girl watching death from her home. Other countries using religion for suicidal intentions, had the U.S livid. I remember the day people being buried under buildings. Couples looking for one another, the sight was chilling. Tears with outrage, Fear coming face to face, buildings falling out of place. Commotion takes place while the lens is recording. Millions of people will never forget the horror.

Political Fever.
Things in the universe are starting to get through to us. Our

president is a white supremacist that's the realest. Walking down the street as were marching for our children. Seven-hundred families have yet to be united. Deported all over the world, now we can't find them. A father from Honduras was stuck in the forest. We're sitting around our televisions watching them report it.

I paused for a second while I realized this revelation. Reflecting on the Great Depression, oppression is still taking up a section, in our government, everything is evident. CNN taking a cut while the cameras continue rolling. Companies are about to make a profit off cloning genes, I heard they want your DNA from Ancestry. Be careful because the government is watching too. Canadian immigrant officials use this as a tool.

Political fever stays away from the non-believers. I'm spitting only facts; This country is a wasteland. Shout out to brent, never too late to highlight greatness. Praising a president whose toupee turned on the wrong side. All jokes aside, this country is not doing right. Last thing I heard was a cop walked in and shot two times. In the wrong apartment, that brother was in his own place. After snooping around the police told the media that paraphernalia was found.

Are we really going to act as if paraphernalia was the reason he got shot down.

Another cold case with excuses about race. Forget a conversation, this is wrong in many ways. Lies from the news reels continue every day. If tragedy had groupies, it's the ones watching the news feeds. I heard she was convicted; I will not say her name, she earned enough fame. Round of applause for the officers that were involved. Our people deserve justice when were shot to death without cause. Political Fever do not turn into a non-believer.

Gun to the head
(Mind Vs Reality)
Waking up this morning feeling all of these emotions. I jumped in the shower & noticed I'm disappointed. Never expected these situations to take notice. Now my mind is frazzled & my life is steadily coasting. Making certain efforts just to do something better. Now life has changed paths. While it caught you off guard your stuck paying the cost.

Staring at the gun, wondering how far your mind will let you run. Cock that thang back and blow your mind off the map. Open your eyes, the piece is still in your lap. Open your eyes, the pistol was never loaded. Open your eyes, you know your momma will miss you. Open your eyes, I know you feel pain inside, but you care about your life. Your mind was opened because reality is fluid. Yielding to external pressures your far from being settled in this life. Stability is a stretch I cannot tell you What comes next. Life will knock you out in a few seconds I can attest. Stay in the bout, pick yourself up off the ground.

Hit a home run and stood tall on the mound. You will go the distance you can figure this out. Mind vs reality your always player one. Gun to the head I cannot do this anymore. Think about your friends, the people you love most.

Always make amends and keep your loved ones close. Suicide will hurt you to the core for sure. Fight against this world, fight against them breaking you down anymore. Do not let your thoughts creep in when you're feeling alone. Appreciate things more and continue your affirmations. Find time for yourself do not focus on the noise.

I promise it's ok to put that cigarette down. I think it is time to move on from that relationship now. The lint in your pocket is not forever, I promise. Find your passions and put in effort it will last you. If you are not listening, then maybe this will pass you. Death is inevitable, try to live your life and leave the past behind. You'll find your piece of heaven somewhere in the timeline. Peace & love to all the drug addicts! Addiction is deep, self-worth is all we need. I pray for our sins in its entirety. I appreciate you all for reading these words that I speak.

SREA

(Staying Real. Educated. And Authentic.)

SREA has been me since I was in my teens. Discovered my gift after my father left the scene. Exchange of energy's writing kept my father with me. Then I grew up and found structure in quality. Quantity started to grow as my creativeness unfolded. Sitting as a little girl writing as I'm told.

The fear, the trauma and loneliness implode, sucked into another world growing as my own. Taking lessons from their and creating my own zone. Approaching reality as I sit on a thrown. Taking in experiences that you might never know. Writing it all down so I can be better than before. Consistent with the craft so my word play is getting better. Telling stories that I live every day. Never worried because my heart will lead the way. That's the joy I'm living with, always been authentic there's no duplicating this. Never graduated college but I am holding some knowledge. Proof of completion was not the piece of paper I received. I can admit not having a degree does not bother me. But working in this world shows within these companies.

I'll never speak a word with zero intelligence. I will do my research and I'll show you the evidence. Self-education has brought me relevance. I'm blessed to be real, that's something you cannot teach. I get these words from God, that's been my protection. Believing in my odds I had to redirect it. I feel as if I'm feigning but my dream is in reach. The luxury will come I want the inspiration. Where I come from there will be no debating. I clearly see a theme; I am the new regime. SREA represents everything I mean. SREA represents individuality.

Chasing.

Woke up this morning with thoughts on my mind. Chasing these highs, every single time. Caught in the middle of my mind & reality. Thinking about these situations, urgency is not forsaken. Planning things out but I never find an ending. I say things out loud, but my actions are in doubt.

Chasing memories. I lived as a young girl realizing my dreams. Vaster than the planes or the galaxies we see. Chasing adolescent just a moment in her presences. She chased imagination with a taste for the creatives. We're living everyday just to start all over again. Why do we pretend? we're chasing from within, my time has been spent, dealing with this nonsense.

This world is a contest, I'm always a contestant. Too Many blessings someone's watching me from heaven. The cycle of an ending always chasing what's repeating. Trying to get a grip on life as I figure out what's right. Always in my head hoping that the end is in sight.

Twenty-nine years old age will hang you by a noose. All these expectations but time to me is aloof. Never even considered growing up, that's the truth. Chasing creativity, It's different than our being. Mentally, physically, it takes control of me.

The Mind of the Disgusting.

Wouldn't you say we all have urges towards something? Mental, spiritual and physical. Everything we are starts with the mind. Everything we want starts with a thought or vision. Personally, experiencing a situation that was unforgettable. Now our lives are fast tracked on this trajectory. Ten years later and it's just a memory.

The Mind of the Disgusting.

How will I dissect the wrong choice? How can we call life a journey when we categorize choices? Even as children, that liberty is taken so freely, even if we need it. Tell me that you understand the outline of what I'm saying. The formation of our mentality may be deceiving. Thinking we know who we are because of what we're receiving. Adolescents are being pulled towards believing.

The Mind of the Disgusting.

There's always beauty in the struggle. Despite what it may look like. There is a fire inside you that burns bright. I pray that you just look inside. I pray that you leave the drugs alone permanently. You're fearing yourself and you're not the only one. The thoughts your mind tell you will never end on its own. Even a sober mind has battles navigating right from wrong.

The Mind of the Disgusting.

He walks this life thinking that the nine-millimeter will save him. He survived a few times; now he is laying low. He and the Homies did a job a few days ago. Dodging the police and the niggas that they stole from. They are living life on the edge just to get some bread. Running for their life as they sacrifice. Fun does not exist; The opposite of bliss, it's chaos and the streets are the ones that their playing with. Bullet holes in snap backs damn, they barely missed.

The Mind of the Disgusting.

The room is always colder at night. You make sure everyone is asleep before you begin to creep. I can hear the hallway floors creaking as you sneak. Trying to surprise me but my smile is in hiding. You're sick mentally to even anticipate my excitement. Everything you do creates the silence of my tears. We both know my options are limited while I'm here.

Night gown on and I'm seventeen years old. Age is the reason why he preys on me alone. The routine never changes. He has a hard on as soon as he approaches. Undressing himself as he makes his way into my bed. He is not fit to be a parent. Collecting checks as a guardian in the foster care system. Living as a low life seems be his mission. Stuck in this hell and I'm not allowed to prosper. We met with a couple last week for adoption. I overheard part of their conversation. He called me his daughter and I was blown away. The night before he told me,

"All I want you to do is open your legs slowly." Never been adopted, why would they bother? A seventeen-year-old who's not interested in college. A year and some change, that's how long he's been behind me. Manipulated into thinking that I really like it. A new set of kids are already making their palates. The last to be adopted someone please explain the logic.

The Mind of the Disgusting.

She sneaks out of the house every night. Once her mother's boyfriend arrives, she climbs out the window. Walking by herself blowing California's best. Free to the night to do whatever she likes. She waited up the street for her ride in her thoughts. Leaning against the bench at the bus stop her stomach starts to sink. Fluttering emotions, her heart could skip a beat. Calm like the ocean as they flow through a world filled with love.

Memories are few, still her spirit floats above. Jenny's ride has arrived with her high beams on. Windows slightly cracked as she pulls up on the side of the curb. The doors unlocked automatically. Jenny and Monica get the pleasantries out the way as she takes a seat. Her friend Monica volunteered to drive tonight. The host of the party is Monica's boyfriend's sister. Ty is her name, so they'll receive free admission. Music is blasting in her Mercedes Benz CLS. She's hitting all the turns as we approach the freeway entrance. They're both aware that the drive to the party is a mission.

All Jenny can think about is Mya and what she's wearing. How she can approach her when she can't control her bearings. Just this ride alone has her thoughts in a frenzy. Waited for this moment just so Jenny could take the lead. Making this happen without distractions is appealing. Coming out the closet with a girlfriend to her mother. Mya is not the only reason Jenny chose to pursue.

She needs her respect despite her families' judgements. Screaming to the world that a lesbian is coming. Her mother is disrespectful. Asking a slew of questions while ignoring what her daughters wants. Seems to be forgetful, never conversed about her boundaries or principles. Never acknowledged that she is her own individual.

The Mind of The Disgusting.

"Handcuffed to the bed as he injects, her eyes roll to the back of her head. Her head is slumped to the side, she's out for the night. He takes his clothes off and presses record. Their faces will be blurred as his penis explores. Hours after his exploration he uncuffs her from the bed. Still zoned out but she's sleep instead. The high is wearing off, she should wake up soon.

He puts his clothes back on and turns the camera off. Recording from a phone as he saves the file. Looking back at her just as a precaution. Walking up the stairs towards his basement door. Leaving her to sleep, he opens and closes the door gently. He turns around to lock the padlock, then continues to lock both sliding latch locks that sit right on top.

He begins to walk down a hallway to yet another door. He knocks three times and waits patiently. Looking through the peep hole he can hear conversations. The doorknob was removed because of complications. The girl in the basement is a runaway, she used to pick the locks and unscrew vents just to get away. My boss refused to tolerate, now she is in the basement.

Before she had a nice room, and meals that would come daily. Now all she sees is big sweaty men locking her to beds. Maybe she'll get a drink of water but only a sip. My boss is a vicious man, very vulgar with his attempts. He had her drinking semen from the tip of his. Anyways I'm just a witness who works for the man. How do you think I know this? I'm the one who babysits. If I give her the wrong attention, then it's off with my head. So much goes on in this place I'm done holding it in.

I could turn them in, but my family would be killed. I know he's only one man, but his reach goes beyond these hills. His life could be a movie, he's legendary here. By the way my name is Maurice, my apologies for the late introduction.

We need to get going with this story if you want to try and help me. I was able to get the girls' name by the way, like you told me. She goes by Chelsey, she's eighteen years old and suffers from diabetes. My boss has been taking care of her, he gives her insulin. Right before their sessions, he helps her to inject it."

Dr Sanchez responds by saying, "Thank you, Maurice, that's all the information I need. I'll make some calls before our session next week. You need to spend time with your depression immediately. Journal about your feelings and how you're thinking presently. Let go of your past and the judgements that you're feeling. Stay aware of your surroundings, remember to think positive. Finally, you need to find another job Maurice.

"Kidnapping and rape? You're involving yourself in illegal activities. I don't want you to be behind bars because of association. Anybody can be associated; Do you understand what I'm saying? Do not allow poor judgment to take away your freedom.

Do not allow fear to keep you where you're seated. That's why you came here on a Wednesday with a gun? I can tell by your stance Maurice. I can also see the bulge in your pants." Maurice starts apologizing to Dr. Sanchez.

"My life is a mess, and my days are reckless.
Cabinets full of empty liquor bottles,
Dr. I'm drowning."
Dr Sanchez said, "hang in there Maurice, don't quit on your journey."

Missing.

She drove her Honda Accord to the store early in the morning. Grabbed a bite to eat and a coffee, still half sleep this happens too often. She paid at the register and the cashier was eyeing her. This happens every time she's not tripping on this man though. She's waving goodbye as they locked eyes, she's walking out the door. Approaching her car, she sees a van that was not there before.

No other customers were inside, plus the cashier's car was parked right Next to hers. She opened her car door and hopped in quickly. Whipped it back accordingly as if it was a stick shift. A cigarette was needed because her nerves screamed panic. On her way to class her homegirl started calling. Her Bluetooth was broken, and she knew it was important. Pulled over real fast so she could hear the entire story. The gear was in park, she proceeded to answer the phone like,

"Girl Wasssssuuuuupp!"
"Girl what happened to you?
"What happened with you and Jacob?"
Before she could answer her friends incoming questions, The call dropped unexpectedly. She pressed redial and her friend answered excitedly.

"Hello?" "Yes girl, let me tell you what happened to me." Talking nonstop, Jasmine was unaware that the call dropped again.
Unaware of her surroundings, with the phone to her ear. The call back came in, startled by the phone's vibration, she answered it. She never took a breath and never said hello. Her friend was on the other

end listening in close. Muffled sounds coming into the receiver now. Uncomfortable with her friend's silence she started yelling out. Jasmine started screaming in the background until the phone hung up. The phone clicked and her friend dialed nine, one, one.

NIP "Niggas in Power."
Damn this hurt me deeply, seeing the news reels last week. A man that was a king! African descent this man was everything. Caught up at his shop and the results we all know about. I wrote this one week after Sunday April first, two thousand and nineteen. Tears start to stream down as I'm sitting going wild. Questioning the courage of the people running out.

Yes, I watched the video of his body on that gurney. Everything makes sense, six shots that did not miss. He rolled with the sixties and Westbrook gave him three twenties. Thirty-three years old, three plus three equals six. Yes, he died violently his spirit still exist. Rest In Peace Nip you was a Crip with so much Power. Your mind just devoured all this information in this world. Shout out to your little girl, her silence spoke volumes. Niggas in power on the front lines that was you.

Wasn't afraid to speak your mind you told the truth. Black fist in the air, rooting for you dude. All hail respect, you connected with your roots. Thinking of technology, parolees and gang members. Owning your own property, that strip mall is a legacy. Malcom X type of thing, a Martin Luther King Dream. All the words that I've said can't deflect the shot to the head. Now I'm looking up ahead empowered in my own right. No disrespect, I am committed to painting his picture with a light. Acknowledging how he went out unfortunately, a brother took this man's life. I'm looking at my melanin just shaking my head. Understanding that we come from the same descent. Niggas in power really need to represent. Just follow Nipsey Hussle in his footsteps. Remember that our people are not done yet. The battle was not won, and the war still carries on.

MR.

Chadwick Boseman, I did not know you, but still I felt a closeness. Looking into your eyes during one of your performances; My brother, you blessed this world so gracefully. Giving inspiration to people like you and me. A Denzel or a Sidney portier, an Ava Duverney. I knew you were here to stay. The creativity and the artistry that prevailed with you on screen. Thurgood Marshall's, Jackie Robinson's and Black Panthers. Those were some of the acts that stood out to me. Now I'm standing here while the world is telling me, cancer got you beat.

This is not a defeat, my apologies I didn't write this to talk negatively. We must make it known; A piece of our culture is now fucking gone. My apologies, this brings the anger out of me. Allow me to watch my mouth while I salute this king. I do this out of respect, money and fame would never make me hesitate. Money and fame are brainwashing our youth today.

The inspiration you've given to men and women, to the people, to the children, to black and our history; You are reminding us of a vision to dream. You remind us that a struggle doesn't mean a thing. You reminded us that being black is a thing. Please spread your wings and know your fans still believe. We salute you, King! Please Rest in peace.

Kanye West

The truth is in his eyes. His opinions I cannot oblige. He might have demons by his side. He might be looking for the light. He's caught in the moments, stuck in the present time, Ideas blasting from his mind. We are Blessed to have him. His music is classical. Created his own fashion and his production will outlast us.

Shout out to the pastors, rejecting all his money but continue to comment even faster. Politics has people thinking backwards. Shout out to Kanye I'm just a fan with a pen. This does not support the shenanigans but then again, maybe this is the real Mr. West. This is the same man that put the music industry in check. No disrespect, I know that line might have an adverse impact. I can see the genius inside of ye', I can relate to your mentality. I would never pity you; You're sailing at a higher view. The words that you speak are integrated in lessons plans at universities.

Watching destruction in the media but I chose not to worry. Shoutout to Sunday service, I was unable to attend but I saw clips of the choir blowing. The essence of churchy was captured, I was watching kevonstage while playing, "The College dropout." I wrote all this to say that you're my idol ye'. Creatively you inspired me to never quit. A moment of silence for his mother's spirit. Donda is the reason that your undisputed.

Welcome Back

I possess gratitude. My journey through this life comes with a positive attitude. I refuse to worry when the message goes silent. As if my mind was abandoned. As a creator you would think I could not manage. Without creativity inspiration is off balance.

I play with my imagination but that's not always the answer. Staying quiet as I wait for the riot. Too much energy inside of me, I cannot stop it. Spewing creativity my poetry has landed. Nothing of this magnitude will ever be abandoned. Call it writers block but my words come from above. Welcoming myself back I'm never falling off.

Thank you, momma.

All the words that I've said I can say them again. Your love is time-less, and I understood that back then. We remember the tragedies. The pain that happened gradually. You might have thought it was hard for me, dealing with you as a child see; I love you for who you are and the actions that were involved.

The pain that we suffered shaped you into a superstar. I was there when you first received your wings. Now you're flying high above the Maldives accordingly. Courage on your shoulder with a strong beating heart. I know dad would be proud, you learned to stand on your own.

All I can say is thank you for bringing me along. A higher power brought me here so I could watch you carry on.

When I was a child, I could tell you felt alone. I never gave up on you because our spirit kept us going. Now I'm looking back, just thanking God for what he did. He gave you so much strength because you never gave in. It is a new day; I can see You're living your life and I know it feels great.

As you get older just know I'm cherishing your days. When I'm not with you I smile, because you're ok. I'd never trade you in your special in many ways. The blessing that always gives; I speak for all of your kids when I say these words like this. Thank you for the sacrifices and everything else you did. From the bottom of our hearts, we love you and that's real.

Own It.

I'm struggling right now but I own it. In my past life I stole people's money, groceries and weed; Whatever was close to me. I'm grateful for this day, I stopped awhile back. Walking a straight line is more challenging than it sounds. When I was in college, I skipped class a lot. Chasing young women just to get a little attention.

Smoking so much weed I do not remember the semester. A lot of feelings involved my mother had breast cancer. Not passing my classes I was doing all the extras. Looking back now I would never think to regret it. I've never been decisive; I struggle on a daily when I try to make my mind up.

Some call this a flaw, but I look at it as if I'm hitting birdies not pars. No matter what they say I know I deserve the applause. Owning who I am as a person is my trophy. Loving all my flaws, staying ready for controversy. Looking up above knowing my lord will have mercy. Taking small steps trying to stretch to the next. Knowing that I'm blessed, finding patience in distress. Every situation comes to me like a test. Knowing if I fail the repercussions will prevail.

Healthy.

This world has people tripping on something heavy. Slipping with my medication, I never keep it steady. Looking up ahead I know that death will be ready. Never want to be scared, how I tend to live is not healthy do you understand?

I smoke a lot of weed so my mind tends to ease. My thoughts can get deep, what's the reason that I breath? Smoking black and mild's while my heart was ripped to pieces. Damn it's been a while since karma came to meet me. I'm looking all around as silence is there to greet me. How'd I get here in twenty-eight years?

Never will I complain, the knowledge in between my ears is lengthy, get a pen. Still breathing on this plane, I'm just trying to make my name. Solidifying myself was always in the plan.
God has his or her eye on this superstar fam.

I can never explain all the gratitude I have. Moved past depression, that always kept me down. When I was a child, my father opened his wings. Learning to forgive life for a broken reality. opening my eyes every day that I breath. Having healthy thoughts pushes me within my peace.

Yin & Yang.

Resisting temptation, my back against the wall, I don't know if I'm going to make it. Selling myself out just so I can live daily. Callus on my hands and my body aching like crazy. Call it a complaint but my body is a temple. Misery is real, this is why I stay spiritual. A system of disease, physically we should be free. Training my mental as I stretch intellectually.

Shadow.

My Quality of life is important. I want to live life with a purpose. Forgive me for my mistakes I was hurting. There's still a lot to learn on this journey. I fear regret, every moment is not correct. Lessons are objective and I can't change without them.

They'll dictate your life like a theme to an event. Nothing can go right if you can't shake that chip. Shoulders holding weight, did you learn from your mistakes? Thinking people see you the same, going in circles is not progressive, breaking these chains by applying pressure. I'm unhinged in my mind I'm just trying to be sane.

Struggling with life seems to always point to race. If I was Caucasian would America show its face? Struggling with your identity, who can you blame? Avidly searching for something else on this plain. Reaching for the sky, how can I obtain, going past the stars, watch what I gain.

Original.

Almond Butter on the tip of my tongue. No cookies today I decided to change up. Another weekend Cali sun hanging tough. Cool breeze sneaking in between the palm trees. I'm thanking God for another day as I lay back. New seeds in my garden, be patient as the roots attach.

Private letters to Mother Nature. Never needing any favors, I just want to say hello. Factual living this life is all I know. All over the globe, one day I'll hit the rode jack. Spiritually in cursive my words travel like earwax. I am certain the door is open on the surface. Assertion has my manifestations working.

Purposely mystic, searching for a deity, answers from a distance, persistent with the vision. Obsessive with the prayers, I'm not kidding.

Caring too much, I'm ready to lift my voice. Carrying the torch, just watch your girl make some noise. Share with the world what I have in stores.

Merchandise me I'm worth every penny. One day you'll realize I'm more important than Hennessy. Temporary solutions will not change generations. Intellectual restitution is not a real thing. Another free-style as I ring your ears now. That was your decision dreaming was never out of style.

Taking my crown and stepping out of endless cycles. Diving far out where tomorrow is never promised. Recycling old habits, but nobody's perfect. I think I can manage, even if I'm hurting. Throwing out my baggage, it's garbage you heard me? Standing on the edge every time that's for certain. Maybe I'll try again, that's a lie filled with purpose.

Cold Walks: Hers & His.
His.
Two or three hours later and he was still driving. Pistol in his lap he wants to knock her cap back. Still, he's relaxed sitting back bumping speakers in his lac. Windows cracked as he cruises in the city Looking for a bitch named Whitney. Back at the house he got some news that wasn't pretty.

It made him feel empty and this nigga is not forgiving. Turn your back on him and that'll be just the beginning. Betrayal is the knife that keeps on digging, hearing this information about the woman who was supposed to bare his children. Now this man's livid, he's getting played by an opportunist. His homie Adam called him up saying some stuff that didn't add up.

"Aye Elijah I swear to God I saw your chick downtown. She had a red dress on with good shoes, bussing it down. The nigga she was with was wearing like a Tom Ford suit and a Rolex my nigga." His reaction was baffling, "I just spoke to her my nigga, I know her schedule, I know about the things she probably doesn't even know. "Adam's response, "bro she is cheating on the low. Your girl is a hoe and you've known that from the jump. Remember that time when we both wanted to hump?" "Yea Adam what's your point?" "My point is that she's a hoe bro,

but she gave me consent that night we were off the patron. Remember her mom and dad had redone their vowels and dipped out of town? After the party we went back to her house. We all took some shots, and then you guys started tonguing each other down. Later that night you and rich passed out. We were alone and had time to talk. Obviously, we were drunk, but she was down with it. Apparently, you were not, so it never came to fruition. "Are you sure you saw her downtown? "Yes Elijah, I did. She was having a private lunch. They both stood up and headed out the door. The only reason she was seen was because she stood up. I wasn't looking for her at all! I was in the middle of the city with my girl Brittany. We decided to stay and talk after we finished eating. We got there as they were leaving,

I saw Whitney and she was just smiling and cheesing." Elijah could not believe it. "Damn my nigga I appreciate you for keeping things real. I'm not even upset about what happened in the past. All I want to do is bust that bitch in the mouth." Adam shook his head, "Calm down my boy, we both know she for the streets."

"Don't get found guilty because this trick is worth nothing." Elijah insisted, "bro let me sit for a minute, my mind is spinning. I'm definitely not thinking clearly." Adam said, "I got you, hit me my nigga and be responsible. "Alight my boy, one." Adam said, "one."

He could not believe it; His rage was slowly creeping. Thinking and thinking he got in the car twisted. Hours later he reminisces about the conversation. He turns the music down he's passing new places now. Chrome against the wheel left hand it while he steers. Whitneys on his mind he's ready to shoot her when it's time. Just two in the clip luck better be on his side.

Hers.

Laying in his bed with these thoughts on her mind. The call was unexpected, he just wanted to spend some time. She was running errands until he happened to hit her line. Butterflies arrived when he spoke and said "hi." A short exchange of words created a situation.

The conversation ended with a subtle invitation. Dine in or dine out, we should get some food right now. Agreeing to meet, she hopes for some privacy. Fifteen minutes later and she's parking her Mercedes. Chilling in the cut, she called him to check his status. "Hello?", "hi, I just pulled in."

"I'm five minutes away just meet me at the door, ok?" "Ok." Getting off the phone to add a touch to her makeup. Checking in the mirror as she rubs her lips together. Satisfied with her look she's preparing to exit the vehicle. Stepping out in heels as her pedicure was on display, manicure on her hands with acrylic nails she came to slay. Trying to avoid messing up her nails ok! she slammed the Benz.

She took a deep breath and had a slight feeling. Thinking of Elijah those thoughts became chilling. Walking across the parking lot as if it is a runway. Strutting her stuff hard in a dress that's tightly fitted. Being a baddie is the strategy to get his attention. Elijah is still on her mind, but time is of the essence. She knows she lied to him and that nigga coming with it. Ignoring her thoughts, she's patiently waiting by the door. Gazing around towards the parking lot entrance. A 2022 Bentley continental GTC convertible is pulling in swiftly.

All Black with the rims matching, looking pretty. He cruises past the entrance and pulls up to the valet. The car door is opened for him as he greets the attendant. The attendant starts speaking, "Good afternoon, sir, how are you doing on this fine weekend?" I'm doing good boy! I like that suit that you are wearing.

"I appreciate that sir, only the nicest for Dave McLarin." He smirked at his statement and put $50 in his square pocket. The boy was in shock, stuttering a thank you but Dave was already gone. Towering to some, Whitney stood 5'8 but today she had her heels on. About 5'11 when you add three inches into the equation. Starring with anticipation, Dave approaches her with a hand full of roses. A smile arose as her lips curved upward. She raised the bouquet up to her nose and inhaled deeply. Thinking to herself this was the gesture she needed.

"Thank you, this was very nice of you. I told you that I like you, all I do is think of you." "Whitney starts blushing, avoiding eye contact she caresses her rose petals. Dave continues, "I made reservations so our table should be ready. When I eat here, I only sit in VIP. Fogo de Chao is delicious Brazilian eatery."

Dave wrapped his arm around her waist as he guided the way. Checking in with the doorman there was no trouble finding his name. A waiter escorted them to where they were going to sit. In the back of the restaurant, the seating was exclusive. Obviously, this man has the money to do this.

Whitney was speechless, she only met him a few times during the NBA season. A childhood friend dances for the Los Angeles Lakers. Whitney believes that she's smashing one of the players, she gave her tickets to a couple playoff games last year. She thinks he's an agent, he manages careers. A little doubtful but she will find out while she's here.

Internal Exposure.
Screaming to those who don't believe. Why do you make this mistake so willingly? Sounding so silly, I cannot comprehend with a dummy. Still they calling me a bum, where did that come from? Assuming

conditions is normal where I come from. Black on black crime is the life in my culture.

In my life I get side eyes from the vultures. Questioning decisions but it's fitting for my position. I know I'm different, to those who did not reach out understand I can't forget it. Uncomfortable situations have me itching like an addict. Understand, it's something vicious. Like a monk in a temple, I was resorting back to my center. I also needed cleansing to reframe my spirit. Searching for breadcrumbs as I begin to re-center.

All I hear is bitchin' close your jaw before I get it. Habits are being formed by judging me and how I'm living. My sister is my sponsor, she uplifts my vision. Telling me to go harder is the blessing I've been given. No apologies please, I'm not encouraging you to reach out to me.

Scissors in my hand I'm cutting strings finally. What is family? Speaking organically is this how it's supposed to be? I have all the drive in the world, but my motor is blowing out. Born to be extraordinary regardless of being noticed. This is the notice; Time is ticking on this explosive. This is just the first of many internal exposures.

The End/Thank You.

We have reached the end. I would like to thank my family, exes and acquaintances for the inspiration. I would like to thank myself for taking a chance and believing in my abilities. Shout out to my supporters! This is the first edition to a new beginning Stay tuned, there's more to come.

Youtube-tatyana roscoe
Instagram-@authenticrenaissance21
@Roscoephotog21
Email-tatyanaroscoe6@gmail.com
Tik Tok- Taty
Website coming soon.
Follow me for updates.